Talking to

Artists

Talking to Programmers

How to Get Programmers and Artists Communicating

Talking to

Artists

Talking to Programmers

How to Get Programmers and Artists Communicating

Wendy Despain

CRC Press
Taylor & Francis Group
Boca Raton   London   New York

CRC Press is an imprint of the
Taylor & Francis Group, an **informa** business

AN A K PETERS BOOK

CRC Press
Taylor & Francis Group
6000 Broken Sound Parkway NW, Suite 300
Boca Raton, FL 33487-2742

Printed on acid-free paper
Version Date: 20161107

International Standard Book Number-13: 978-1-4987-0073-3 (Paperback)

Library of Congress Cataloging-in-Publication Data

Names: Despain, Wendy, author.
Title: Talking to artists, talking to programmers : how to get programmers and artists communicating / by Wendy Despain.
Description: Boca Raton, FL : CRC Press, Taylor & Francis Group, 2016. | Includes bibliographical references and index.
Identifiers: LCCN 2016030818| ISBN 9781498700733 (pbk. : alk. paper) | ISBN 9781315381626 (ebook : alk. paper)
Subjects: LCSH: Interpersonal communication. | Intergroup relations. | Artists--Professional relationships. | Computer programmers--Professional relationships. | Video games industry--Social aspects.
Classification: LCC HM1166 .D48 2016 | DDC 302.3--dc23
LC record available at https://lccn.loc.gov/2016030818

Visit the Taylor & Francis Web site at
http://www.taylorandfrancis.com

and the CRC Press Web site at
http://www.crcpress.com

Printed and bound in the United States of America by
Edwards Brothers Malloy on sustainably sourced paper

Contents

Preface: Talking to Artists

Artists and programmers often work together on complex projects in stressful environments and things don't always go smoothly. Miscommunication and misunderstandings are common as these two disciplines often use the same words to mean different things when they talk to each other. Unintentional slights can turn into long-held grudges and productivity grinds to a crawl.

This book can help anyone who wants to improve communication with artists and programmers. It's set up like a foreign language dictionary, so it addresses the cultural norms, attitudes, and customs surrounding the words each group uses, so you'll know not just what the words in the glossary mean, you'll know why they're used that way and how to get communication flowing again.

It addresses common reasons for communication problems between these two groups and provides specific suggestions for solutions. The unusual format allows for each side to be given equal weight—learn how to talk to artists starting on one side of this book, turn it over and learn how to talk to programmers. The whole book stresses the things artists and programmers have in common.

Focused primarily on videogame developers, it also applies to other fields where tech and art have to work together, including web developers and teams building mobile apps. This book can help anyone who wants to communicate better with programmers or artists.

Acknowledgments

I would like to thank all the people who encouraged me to write this book, especially Aerin Artessa, the artist who urged me to finish as soon as possible. I would also like to thank all those—both artists and programmers—who reviewed the material and provided case studies. Especially when you pointed out the places where I was sounding mean instead of blunt. I deeply appreciate your honesty and hope I have rectified the problems. There are also many students, who will remain anonymous, who helped me spot patterns and clarify solutions as we worked through these situations on their teams. I also appreciate all the people who made the clever cover on the book everything it is—from the editorial team who believed in my vision to Mario Rodriguez who helped me practice what I am preaching. And finally, I would like to thank Giles Schildt, former Director of Game Development for SJ Games, who reviewed the manuscript thoroughly for me and made excellent suggestions.

Author

Wendy Despain is a videogame writer and narrative designer with more than a decade of experience spearheading digital media projects. She has worked with teams around the world as a team leader, designer and consultant on console and PC games, mobile apps, online experiences, alternate reality games (ARG), and augmented reality. Some of her credits include an ARG for *Gene Roddenberry's Andromeda*, *Jetset Secrets* on Facebook, and *Fusion Fall* from Cartoon Network. She is currently teaching team building and production strategies at SMU Guildhall in Plano, TX. Her other books include *Professional Techniques for Videogame Writing* (AK Peters/CRC Press, 2008), *Writing For Videogame Genres: From FPS to RPG* (AK Peters/CRC Press, 2009), and *100 Principles of Game Design* (New Riders, 2012).

① Making Sense
Framing the Conversation

Communicating with artists can be hard. They sometimes seem standoffish, oversensitive, and dramatic. It's easy to feel like talking to them is pointless or even counterproductive, but it doesn't have to be that way. Artists are human too, and they want to talk. This book will help untangle communication lines, provide concrete solutions, and backup plans.

Artists assigned to technical projects—especially software projects—frequently feel isolated, misunderstood, and underappreciated. They often come from a significantly different educational background and social group than every other member of the team. If more than one artist is assigned to a project, they tend to stay close to each other, watching each other's backs like tourists on a strange planet.

When they're alone together, they speak a native language with familiar-sounding words, but they have meanings nobody outside their group understands. Drop one of these words in your own feedback at some point and the results are often bewildering. At the same time, the artists complain about being given vague feedback, when you're just trying to express something you don't quite understand about what's missing or wrong.

Many times there will be one or two people—sometimes from within the ranks of the artists, sometimes a project manager or director, very rarely a programmer—these people become cross-departmental translators. Somehow they manage to make themselves understand when talking to both artists and more technically minded people. Many large teams depend on these translators to keep projects moving forward and consider this the best solution to the problem.

It's not a bad solution. And if you want to become that translator for your team, this book can help you get there. There are some downsides, though. This translator role is often informal, underappreciated, and occasionally goes completely unrecognized.

And any solution with a single point of failure is high risk. What if the translator is sick for a few days? What if they get a job somewhere else? What if they aren't on the same page as upper management when it comes to the big-picture vision for this project?

The risks can be mitigated by employing a few more translators, but imagine if entire departments were able to speak each other's language! Even if a translator is out sick for a day, communication can still go on without them. And if one person is having trouble making themselves understand, their coworker could step in and provide another perspective, helping to clarify instead of muddying the waters.

This book is set up to be passed around the office and shared across disciplines. Just like any other foreign language dictionary, there's a side for learning how to speak Art and a side for learning how to speak Tech. One person can study it at a time, or groups can work on it together. But even if you're the only one on the team who is interested in making communication work more smoothly, there are suggestions peppered throughout this book specifically designed for engaging groups in conversations over lunch or ice cream or bagels. These conversation starters can help iron out some of the wrinkles even if nobody else wants to look at this book.

When communication breaks down between departments, the ripple effect can be profound. Sometimes it just means a few individuals have a less-fun job. But many times, it can grow into a constant tension hanging in the air. It can result in meetings turning into bickering sessions and outright feuds developing, where the communication problem looms so large nobody remembers why they're working on this project in the first place. Miscommunication between departments can absolutely destroy an otherwise on-track product.

How to Use This Book

This book is divided up into sections and subsections. The two main sections are mirror images of each other. The Art side and the Tech side both have the same chapter names with the same goals—to teach artists how to speak tech, and techies how to speak art.

Dictionary: Each side of this book includes a dictionary of commonly confused terms. The Art side explains what these terms mean to an artist, and the Tech side explains what these terms mean to a techie. Some suggestions on how to use the dictionary are

- If someone from the art department uses a word in a meeting that you're not quite sure about, look it up in the dictionary.

- Read through page by page to familiarize yourself with the vocabulary so that you can use them correctly when talking to artists.

- If you are tempted to use a specific word when providing feedback to artists, look it up on both sides of the dictionary before using it. Share the definitions with the person you're going to be talking to so you can start out on the same page.

Lunch topics: Throughout this book, there are sidebars that pull out important concepts which can help build bridges across the divide between Art and Tech. They provide suggestions for how to bring up the topic, how to get people

> ## Lunch Topic
> Pick a word from the dictionary and discuss what it means to each of you and how it relates to the project you're working on together.

talking, and onto the same page. These topics don't have to happen over lunch, although food can be a great social lubricant. Bring them up as everyone is standing around the Friday donuts, or when you go out for drinks after a major milestone.

But if you make it an agenda item for a staff meeting, assuming you've got that kind of pull, be careful. These topics can be sensitive and emotional sometimes, and best covered in a casual, nonthreatening environment where people don't feel like they have to defend themselves.

Case studies: Throughout this book are specific, real-world examples of communication breaking down between the Art department and the Tech department. Most of them are verbatim as they were told to me. Some of them have been edited slightly for clarity, while others have had identifying features changed. This isn't about placing blame or shaming. It's about learning from each other and sharing best practices.

Problem-surf: Consider what specific problems your team may be facing right now, and skim through this book looking at subheads and bolded words that relate to your problem. Reading just those sections can help a lot, although it will likely just put a bandage on the problem. To fix the underlying issues, you'll probably need to read the whole book so the sections are in context.

Cover to cover: While this is the traditional way to read a book, it won't quite work this time. If you haven't tried to read the back cover yet ... give it a try now. You'll find there isn't one. To read this book fully, you'll have to pick a side and read to the middle, then turn it over and read to the middle again.

As a programmer, you'll probably find the "Talking to Artists" side of this book to be the most useful. You probably already know quite a bit about how to talk to other programmers. If you want to read that side of this book, you may gain some insights into how artists see you. This might open doors of communication and help solve problems, just because you've learned more about how you are perceived. The same territory is covered on both sides. So if you're curious about the advice being given to artists about how to communicate with you—by all means, dive in to that side of this book.

Study guide: This book can be used in a semiformal or formal learning environment as well. Use it as a textbook in staff training meetings with assigned readings. Lunch topics become group discussion topics.

Gift: Drop it on the desk of the lead artist and tell them you would like to know what they think about it. Try not to just do this as a drive-by thing. Be genuine. Use this book as a gift to help break the ice.

No matter how you use this book, open your mouth and start talking. Just like any foreign language, practice with native speakers is essential in order to become truly fluent. Admit you're learning, and this is all new to you and you'll be surprised how willing artists will be to meet you in the middle for a conversation.

Working Together

Common Problems and Pitfalls, Plus Solutions

Every situation is a little different, but most problems grow from common roots. The difficulties listed here aren't exhaustive, but they are some of the most frequent issues that arise on technical projects with an artistic component.

Consider whether you're currently encountering any of these problems now, or have in the past. Sometimes problems seem to have subsided when really they have just taken a backseat to a larger problem. Other times, temporary solutions are found that provide a period of seeming calm, but in reality they have only delayed and sometimes intensified a later eruption.

The solutions suggested here are not exhaustive, but are intended to provide jumping-off points for finding answers that work in your unique situations. Think of them as seeds to start your brainstorm session, rather than strict prescriptions. Detailed explanations of each cause and effect provide a clear look at the root of the problem, so resolutions can be focused there, rather than smoothing over symptoms temporarily and letting the true problem fester.

Artists are passionate people who care deeply about their work and want very much to make substantive contributions. They genuinely don't want to cause extra problems, and sometimes this means they try to minimize or ignore issues instead of tackling them head-on. New problems crop up because of this and won't go away until the core issue is taken care of.

You may face resistance when trying to solve team difficulties because artists may feel you are attacking a solution they put in place to solve a different problem. Listening, asking questions, and taking the answers to those questions seriously is crucial in this process.

Common Problems from the Art Department

Providing Art That Doesn't Meet Requirements

What it looks like: The art department is churning out assets … but they don't fit the direction decided on for the project, or don't reflect guidance that was established and agreed on. There are several possible reasons for this happening.

- Artists don't like the established direction, and don't feel like their objections have been heard and taken into account.

- The person assigned these tasks is distracted or overworked. They may be rushing through their tasks and not paying attention to the details.

- The person assigned these tasks is not the right person. They don't have the skills to meet the requirements, but they're either unaware of this or unwilling to admit it.

- Requirements or guidelines have been communicated in a way that didn't work for the artists.

- There is a miscommunication about expectations—for instance, if they are providing placeholder art when final art is expected.

What to do about it: One or two assets out of a few dozen that are out of spec can be a simple oversight. However, if it's an endemic problem, or a recurring issue, you'll need to dig down to find out which of the above causes is the root of the problem. Start out with a conversation. Tell the artist the assets don't fit the requirements and provide examples of what you mean. It might help to prepare ahead of time by taking screenshots of several pieces of art and setting them side by side with the requirements they don't fit. Artists are very visual. They use images the way programmers use numbers, and words are often not precise enough to describe art that is incorrect.

Once you have clear explanations for what is out of spec, then ask how it got to that point. Ask if there is something you can do to help. Can you be more clear on the requirements, or help with training? But most of all, be ready to listen. Chances are the artists are not feeling heard in some way.

Art That Meets Requirements, But Doesn't Look Good

What it looks like: Art assets are meeting technical specifications and within the realm of the agreed on direction (for instance, you're not getting pirates when you asked for spaceships) but the quality of the art is just not very good. You know the artists can do better. They just aren't.

What to do about it: Get a second opinion. Find out if you're the only one (or the only department) feeling this way. Compare the work you're getting with competitors. Maybe the art is different from what you expected, but more in line with the larger fashions than you realize. And take a look at the promises the artists have made themselves. What inspiration images are they working from? What have they shown as their target for quality? Do a side-by-side comparison with what was expected versus what was delivered.

If you're still convinced it doesn't measure up, bring these comparisons to the art lead and be ready to

Case Study
Mike Sellers, Lead Designer

On *The Sims 2*, a lot of the art was done by an external art house and ended up being done to many different scales. This didn't matter so much on the original *Sims*, since all the art was flattened to 2D bitmaps before being used.

But when we tried to use the 3D models for *The Sims 2*, it became chaos. It turned out no basic scaling factor had been communicated by the technical team to the art team, and so we had some models that were monstrously huge and some that were uselessly small. We ended up re-doing almost all the art and discarding the old art – an expensive lesson.

explain the differences you're seeing in them. This can be a hard conversation, but it's this or learn to love what your artists are delivering. Those are your only two choices. Either confront them directly with your concerns or let it go, and trust they know what they are doing.

Many times, the artists will be eager to hear feedback on their work and will not be surprised that you're not happy with it. They are rarely happy with their own work, but sometimes have a hard time pinpointing what's wrong. This is where your side-by-side comparisons can be invaluable. Sometimes the artists have lost their way unintentionally. Sometimes they are trying so hard they are afraid to take necessary risks.

Remind the artists why you believe they can do better. Show them work they did that you really liked. The beginning of this conversation might be a blow to their ego, but make sure the end of it is positive and full of encouragement.

Lunch Topic

Try searching for images on the Internet with similar themes. For instance, "party" or "sunset" or "mountain." Bring a selection of these images to your lunch and lay them out on the table. Try to describe just one of these images well enough that your lunch companions can figure out which one you're talking about. Then give the others a turn.

When programmers are describing, only artists can guess the picture. When artists are describing, only programmers can guess.

You will probably find this game to be more challenging than you expect. You may learn new vocabulary words, new ways of explaining what you see, and an appreciation for how much faster you can communicate when you use related pictures when describing art needs.

Revisions That Don't Work

What it looks like: Artists agree to make specific revisions to art assets, but what they deliver doesn't solve the original problem, or introduces new ones.

What to do about it: This is often a sign of miscommunication. Sometimes artists who are feeling a lot of pressure will agree to things they don't like or don't fully understand, just so they can get out of the uncomfortable situation. If artists are not used to doing revisions, or if they are particularly attached to a piece of art, they may not have been able to think clearly when it is being criticized.

Try to avoid telling artists how to solve a problem, and instead show them what the problem is and let them come up with the solution. Many times it helps to break these two conversations into separate meetings. First talk about what isn't working optimally for the art, and make sure everyone understands the problem. Then set up a meeting for talking about solutions later.

Many times the artists will arrive at that meeting with at least one proposal better than what you would have suggested. If they truly understand why the revisions are being requested, they are more likely to follow through on them successfully, and if they come up with the solution themselves there are far fewer opportunities for misunderstandings.

Lateness

What it looks like: This can be individual lateness to meetings or missing deliverable deadlines. Either way, when art is expected to be there, it's just not.

What to do about it: First keep in mind that punctuality is not a common trait for many artists. To a certain extent, this is just going to be a fact of life when working with an art department. Try to be patient about it, and mostly leave this up to the project manager or the department lead if you can. Communicate with that individual about wasted time or frustration.

Missing deliverable deadlines, on the other hand, is a different matter. Professional artists should know how to estimate their work relatively well. It's just a part of doing the job. Of course, everyone runs into unexpected delays, so don't worry about late deliverables from the art department until it becomes a trend. Then sit down with them to look at the process—but make it clear you are wanting to do this to help the artists and the overall project, not because you are trying to find out who to blame.

If the artists see you as trying to help, they will often be quite open about what caused the delays. If they are being hesitant to talk about it, ask if it was something the tech department contributed to. Maybe you are integrating their assets too late in the schedule. Maybe the original specifications weren't delivered soon enough. Be ready to hear that you contributed to the problem. And even if you didn't, the artists will feel like you're on their side if you are open to that possibility.

Help them walk through their processes to find where they are underestimating effort, or making promises they can't deliver on. Make any adjustments you can to help them deliver on time.

Special case: Midnight deadlines and 12:00 a.m. batch jobs can cause a lot of confusion. Artists will think of "Midnight on Thursday" as the minute after 23:59 (11:59 p.m.) Thursday, so your automated process will often run 24 hours earlier than they expect. It's best to avoid midnight and noon as times to schedule batch jobs. It's not worth the confusion and extra communication to try to keep everyone synched up.

Ignoring Pipelines

What it looks like: Working together as a team is often difficult, but clear pipelines and established processes help a lot. When someone on the team ignores these pipelines, it can cause a domino effect with problems coming thick and fast. Artists may be skipping an approval process, or checking in work they haven't fully tested yet. Whatever it is, they're ignoring an established pipeline and the project is paying the price.

What to do about it: First make sure everyone is on the same page about what the pipeline is supposed to be. The art department may be working from an old draft of the policy, or they may have modified it internally without realizing it would impact work beyond their department. So first ask what their pipeline is and compare it to what you think it's supposed to be.

When you encounter differences, ask why it's not happening the established way. Maybe there's a roadblock you're unaware of. Many times artists will try to solve problems on their own without bothering other departments. Sometimes this works beautifully. Sometimes they don't know why a step is required, so they skip it or implement it incorrectly. When you can find these gaps, you can fill them and solve the problem.

If they are skipping steps in the pipeline because they don't understand their significance, take some time to explain the "why" behind the "what." Many technical requirements seem arbitrary to artists, but if you can show them the effect of ignoring them, they will often get on board.

Vague Estimates

What it looks like: Artists estimate their work will take far longer than the available time for the project, or they provide wide ranges— a particular task could take anywhere from 30 minutes to 30 days.

What to do about it: If this is at the very beginning of the project, be patient with them. They will get better at estimating as they get more experience with the ins and outs of this particular project. Wide estimates often mean the artists are in unfamiliar territory in some way. This is a common characteristic of any tech project in the early stages.

If the vague estimates continue to show up well into the project development cycle, something deeper is happening. Very likely, the artists feel like the goalposts keep moving. They still don't have a firm understanding of what they are doing for the project, or they are frustrated with the way the project is changing over time. Sometimes this is because they misunderstand the reason or direction of the changes. Sometimes their objections are not being taken seriously when changes are discussed. Take time to listen to their concerns, and keep them in mind the next time a change is suggested.

However, you'll also need to resist the urge to make decisions about the art workload or processes without consulting them. Don't just assume something you would like to do will put too much pressure on the art department—ask them about it, and be receptive to their responses. Artists often don't like to say "no" to people, so be aware of hesitation in conversation. It often means the artist is

Case Study
Jim Preston, Producer

I remember in the early days of adopting agile there was all sorts of excitement around proper estimation, whether it was t-shirt sizes, Fibonacci numbers or something else. One time a department manager came back from training and announced that the new hotness was using animal sizes to represent effort, from mosquito to whale. The result was a planning session where people honestly debated whether 2 dogs were bigger than one horse, and the question got into discussions of average breed sizes. This nonsense went on for half an hour of serious discussion among normally very intelligent, professional game devs.

uncomfortable, but doesn't want to make other people uncomfortable by sharing their concerns. If you show that you listen, you care about what impact your work has on theirs, and respect their opinions, they will be more willing to speak up about what's bothering them, rather than trying to build in a lot of wiggle room in the timeline while they figure out how to pull off a miracle.

Lost Assets

What it looks like: Artists are creating art assets, but some of them are not making it into the product.

What to do about it: Examine the pipeline. Somewhere, something is going awry. It may be a misunderstanding about how the pipeline is supposed to work (on their end or yours) or it may be a lax approach to following the pipeline. Sometimes this can happen because the artist doesn't understand why they have to take all the steps they are asked to take. "Because then it gets into the final product" can be good enough motivation, but often they don't understand how the step they are skipping contributes to the end goal. They may assume something shows up for the tech department the same way it shows up for them. Or they may not understand how the pipeline works once the asset moves out of their immediate control. Filling in these knowledge gaps can help minimize lost assets in the future.

Case Study
Keith Fuller, Programmer, Leadership Trainer

As a gameplay programmer I worked on a team with a particular artist who—like many others—worked predominantly with a stylus rather than a mouse. Great for art, lousy for precise click-and-drag file management in Windows. Halfway through the day, the network build of our game stopped working—something about missing assets. After a significant period of time passes, with every programmer dedicated to solving the mystery, Stylus meekly approached the lead programmer and explained that—quite a while earlier—he *might* have accidentally dragged the entire asset folder out of its proper location. Where to? Hard to say on an enormous network.

Step 1: Locate asset folder.
Step 2: Return it to its proper location.
Step 3: Explain to Stylus that he will always use a mouse to manipulate files.

Intense Arguments about Minutia

What it looks like: Artists are spending hours arguing about the smallest details—and not creating art.

What to do about it: This behavior often mystifies tech departments. You're not alone. To some degree, this is not really a problem (just a weird thing artists do) as long as they are still meeting their deadlines. The real problem comes in when they are delaying the creation of art assets, or engaging people from other departments and delaying their work.

When an artist is doing this, they are usually trying to wrap their heads around the big picture. They are focusing on edge cases—details—to try to understand where the boundaries are. Some of this is healthy and necessary as the creative process moves along and the project comes into focus. Too much of it means the art department is confused about fundamental design decisions. There is something they do not like or do not understand about the project as a whole.

Sometimes, they know exactly what that is and are eager to talk about it if anybody asks them what the bigger issue is. Sometimes they're not even aware of it themselves, and they need someone to point out that they have been stuck on minutia for far too long. If you push them to think about why this is such a sticking point for them, they may be able to articulate the larger problem. Once that problem is solved, the discussions about tiny details will usually fade.

Silos, Hoarding Information, Internal Competition

What it looks like: Artists getting very upset when someone in the tech department touches the art in any way—adding a post-processing effect, motion blur, particle effect, etc. Even if everyone agrees the effect is great, the art department may get very angry about tech stepping on "their turf" and refuse to allow the tech-created "art" into the final product. They actively harm the project as they defend their territory from the encroachment of people on their own team.

What to do about it: Involve the art department as soon as possible. Don't surprise them with how great the effect looks, instead talk to them about what you would like to try before trying it. If there is

Case Study

Jeff Pobst, Founder and CEO

Our teams at Hidden Path Entertainment sit together cross-discipline (designers next to programmers next to artists who are working on the same area of the game). And for the most part, I think we have an environment where communication issues are not a problem. There will always be "the solution I know how to do" versus the solution that someone else knows how to do with their particular skill set, but that's not too entertaining. Just that when faced with new problems, each person has a better understanding of their area and their tools than the other person's.

But I love the culture that I see where programmers and artists get together and talk about different ways to solve a problem and try to figure out if its easier to solve in content or solve in tech. If anything I see more of the "oh, don't worry I can fix that in art," "no, really I can fix it in code if you'd rather," "Nah that's ok, I can take of this," are you sure, "cause I can fix that for you my way," etc. It's almost like the paralyzation of going through a doorway because people are being so nice to each other and saying "no you go first."

internal competition in the organization, it will raise its ugly head here, and with the help of leads and project managers you can combat it in the early stages before it harms the project.

Some of the best ways to break down silos is to break down the physical barriers that are emblematic of the workflow silos. If you have any control over seating arrangements, consider integrating artists and programmers together into the same workspace. Alternate seating, or otherwise ensure that programmers are sitting right next to artists on a daily basis, not just in a programmer-only pod. Allow feature teams with representatives from multiple departments to sit together. If you don't have control of seating arrangements directly, try making the suggestion to those who do.

Alternatively, when you're working on something coming close to the artist's "turf," take a laptop over near their workspace while you work on that feature. Being physically close to them, asking their opinion, may help them see you as a member of the team, and not an enemy at the gates.

Finally—don't fall into this trap yourself. Technically inclined artists may produce tools, features, and other assets that fall into programmer territory. Hold back your instinct to take offense. Remember that you're all on the same team, working together to make the best end product you can all make. It may seem like commentary or criticism about how you're doing your job, but most of the time those artists are only trying to help, and not trying to show you up at all.

3 The Way We Think

The Artist's Mind

The mind of an artist is an exciting, sometimes chaotic place. New ideas are sparking all the time. It can feel like walking through a room full of live electrical lines with 3 inches of water on the floor. Big ideas and little ideas dance around in dark corners and sometimes jump out and hit the artist with a flash of insight or a fully formed image.

Some artists even foster a sense of disorganization so that different concepts collide with each other in unique and unexpected ways. If their mind is too orderly and constrained, they won't be able to generate images that look interesting, new, and creative.

Art has a messy creative process. Intellectually, an artist may know exactly what they want to produce ... or they may have to get started creating before they really know where they're heading. They aren't given specific guidance along the way—people look over their shoulder and suggest things like "it should have more wow" when nobody knows what that even means.

If artists do manage to settle on a conceptual design before getting to work on the project, they are faced with tools that are so imprecise; it can be very discouraging to try to get the image they have in mind out into the real world. No matter what medium an artist uses, a small tremor or slip of the hand can dramatically change the way a piece looks. And good artists are open to this happening, seeing it as just a part of the process of creation.

They start from nothing and work their way gradually closer and closer to the concept they had in mind when they started. In the beginning, it looks nothing like the original idea. By the end of the process, it may be very close to the concept the artist dreamed up. But it may be completely different and still correct for the project at hand.

This is one reason artists hesitate to show others their work as they go along. If the artist thinks the image isn't yet showing what they intend, feedback from others may not be very helpful. It can't be a team effort until the image comes close to what the artist had in mind to begin with, and that can take a longer time than they expected.

Unlike programming, there is never a distinct "yes this works" or "no this doesn't work." It's all a matter of opinion and style. Since everyone has a different sense of style, there are times when nobody agrees on whether an image meets the requirements or not. There's no bug checker to produce useful reports and no compiler to tell them they're missing a semicolon somewhere.

Artists often feel perpetually lost as they push and pull their very analog process (even digital artists) into a state that can make the most important people happy with the results. They grow gradually more confident in the image as they work on it longer and often feel like it would be even better if they had more time. To them, the stopping point where they need to move on to the next image can seem arbitrary and far too soon for the quality of the work. But there's no definitive way of defending this position. At some point, they just have to trust that the image is good enough for what it needs to be. This can make letting go a hard thing to do.

In team situations, this can sometimes develop into a situation where the artists feel the need to build up walls around their work and avoid sharing it until it's close to finished. This may make them feel better throughout the early stages of the creative process, but it's usually a sign that the feedback loop has a serious problem. If any team hides out too much, they can lose sight of the original vision the whole team is working toward. So communication with artists is essential, but it can also feel like a barrage of negativity to them while the work isn't finished.

Case Study

Amy Beatty, Artist

A lot of confusion can come from the difference between subtractive color theory and additive color theory.

Subtractive color is what you get when you mix pigments (paint, ink, wax, etc.) together. This is what most people feel comfortable with intuitively. It's called subtractive because what you see with pigments is the color of the light that reflects off the pigment. The light that is absorbed is being subtracted from the spectrum. In subtractive color theory, you start with white, and the more color you add, the closer you get to black because the more colors are subtracted from the spectrum of the light that reaches your eyes. Subtractive color is used when painting or creating print assets.

When working with digital colors on a glowing computer screen, you're using additive color rather than subtractive. Additive color begins with black–no colors of light reaching the eye, and as you add more color, you move closer and closer to white–which is when all of the colors of the spectrum reach your eye.

It's important to note that additive and subtractive color systems employ different primary colors, and mixing two colors in additive color will not give you the same result as when you mix the exact same two colors subtractively. Therefore, when designing for print (subtractive color) on a computer screen (additive color) there has to be some mechanism for translating one color system into the other. Often artists who are accustomed to working in subtractive color have difficulty working with computer people who are accustomed to working in hexadecimal additive color because neither side realizes that they are using entirely different color systems in which color mixing just does not behave the same.

When talking to artists, remember to ask questions about the image you're looking at. But make sure feedback sessions are a dialog and not an interrogation. Remember that they may be skilled with the tools at hand, but still very frustrated with the results of their efforts so far. Tell them the things that are good about their work every time you discuss it. Otherwise they hear only that the piece isn't working and may feel like starting over on something that was nearly perfect.

④ Providing Feedback

How to Give Feedback to Artists

Artists working in technical fields get a lot of negative feedback. Their coworkers are usually quite good at explaining what they don't want to see, but have a hard time articulating what it is they are really looking for. Instead of working toward a clear list of requirements, artists usually have to produce an example piece and hear back from colleagues all about how wrong it looks. They make a few changes, show it off again, and hear once again how it still isn't right. This process continues until their team has fewer and fewer negative things to say and may occasionally bring up a positive comment.

Requirements lists for artists usually look like people trying to describe wine. The art must be "fresh, bright, and new." or "deep, realistic, and edgy." This isn't much more helpful than telling a programmer they need to make "a program that runs fast and makes good data."

So when an artist finds someone who is willing to talk about their art in specific terms and provide useful feedback, they count them as a valuable resource. If that person also points out the positive elements of the work now and then, you've got a friend for life (or at least a valuable partner who brings quality work to all their collaborations with you).

Tips for providing feedback:

Point out what you like about the art: If the artists don't know which aspect of the art really hits the mark, it can easily get lost in the next iteration. Even if it feels like you could save time by only pointing out the few things that are wrong—instead of going over all the things that are right—you won't be wasting time or effort by praising the elements that really work. Think of it as identifying the innocent bystanders so they don't get hit when the artist goes in to eliminate the villains.

Say what you mean: Don't use technical terms casually. If you tell an artist that the piece has a "darker hue than you expected," you may be surprised by the changes they make. Learning their vocabulary will give you a wealth of tools.

Prepare ahead: Take some time to really look at the art and think about what you like and dislike. Off-the-cuff reactions are sometimes counterproductive. If an artist won't give you time to think about your responses, focus on the things you like about their piece. Stick to the positive and find a way to deliver the negative after you've both had a chance to think about things for a bit.

Be specific: Avoid using vague terms like "punchy" or "zing." Focus on parts of the piece rather than addressing your feedback to the piece as a whole. If there's something pervasive that's not right, try to put your finger on what that thing is. The tone? The shadows? The lighting?

Bring examples: Show pictures of what you mean by "cheerful" or "spooky." Artists can see specific techniques in these pieces that you may not know how to describe or what the name of it is. If you have more than one example of what you mean, even better.

Be realistic: Keep in mind that art is very subjective and every artist has a slightly different style. Embrace the quirks that your particular artists bring to the project. Don't expect them to do things that are identical to your examples. Trust them to capture the spirit of what's shown to them and translate it through their particular art style into something unique and new.

Speak up: Ask if the artists would like some feedback, and respect them if they say something like "not now." And don't give up. They may be back later to hear what you want to say. Sometimes, everyone else in the team will be happy with the art and you just have to go along with it. But sometimes people just aren't talking about what is on their minds and the artists are starving for some understanding of how their work is fitting in with the overall project.

Case Study

Judy Tyrer, Senior Engineering Manager

I complained early on asking "why can't my artist give me what I asked for?" Andrea Fryer was the biggest help. She asked for my description, and I sent it to her. She then sent me three screenshots of artwork that totally and completely matched my verbal description. Only one of them was what I wanted.

I stopped using words immediately. Now I send montages of the kind of thing I'm trying to communicate. Artists are visual so send them visuals.

5 Taking Feedback

What Do Artists Know About Programming?

It's hard to take feedback from the art department. They focus on trivialities, talk in generalities, and don't know a variable from a compiler. Their feedback still matters.

- The best feedback doesn't come from the most knowledgeable person. It comes from the most attentive person. And artists have a formidable eye for detail. They can't do their jobs without it.

- They are part of the team. Artists have a vested interest in seeing the project do well. They care deeply and will give honest feedback if given a chance and taken seriously. They may not know how to implement their suggestions—or have any idea of how difficult and time-consuming those suggestions might be—but that freedom from thinking about constraints can be invaluable. They will think outside the box and provide new ideas.

- Artists also have a better chance of being able to look at the project from the perspective of the average user. Programmers are locked-in to a particular point of view simply because they have so much experience with technology. Things that are intuitive and self-evident to programmers can be baffling for average users. Artists can throw out a warning flag about these details during production, long before end users get a chance to be confused.

- Artists are highly trained in communicating with visuals. They can spot problems and provide solutions for confusing interfaces, or provide suggestions for making interactions easier to understand.

So don't overlook the valuable resource you have in feedback from the art department.

Decoding Artist Feedback

Just because artists have an important point of view doesn't mean it's easy to understand. Their feedback is often couched in emotion words like, "It just doesn't feel right," or "It makes me angry." They even make up words sometimes to try to get their point across, though this usually doesn't make it any clearer for programmers.

It can be most useful to watch artists interacting with the product, and at the same time, they are talking about their feedback. The words combined with the actions often illuminate the core problem they are trying to describe. For instance, ask them to show you where or how they first noticed the problem. Watch over their shoulder as they walk you through their actions and talk you through their feedback.

While this is going on, also ask them what they expected to happen or how they would like it to work. This can get them to talk more about specifics like speed, timing, and coordination. Resist the urge to tell them that the way it currently works is how it was intended or designed to work. Take advantage of the fact they don't have the inner workings in mind when they are using the systems. This will make their reactions more typical of your end users and can highlight elements that aren't intuitive enough.

Artists assigned to work on your project probably already know you had a plan, and they respect that even though they rarely say it. In their domain, nothing ever works exactly the way they imagined or planned that it would. Getting the image from their brain out into the real world is an imperfect science. So they are in the habit of starting with their best guess and refining from there. They will assume this is your process as well. They aren't trying to say that your plan was bad. They are just expressing how the product functions for them.

When you defend features, they point out by saying they work as intended, the artist doesn't see that as a valid reason for not making changes. Their own work is often criticized for very subjective reasons like taste and style. If the feature they are having trouble with is clunky because it fits into a large, unfinished system of other features, just thank them for their feedback and have them try it again after the interlocking pieces are all in place. They may still have the same issues—or they may not. You won't know until they try it.

Ask questions: Even if their feedback seems pretty clear on the face of it, ask clarifying questions to make sure you're both on the same page. One person's "slow" is another person's "dead."

Take notes: This will make the artists feel like you are really hearing what they have to say, even if you don't end up doing what they suggest. If you write down their feedback, it will feel to them like you gave their opinion a fair chance.

Listen for the message: Artists sometimes try to offer solutions to problems, thinking they are being helpful. Try to get them to focus more on the experience they are having and what they don't like about it. Assure them that this is what you're looking for, just wanting to know what they think of what you've made, so you can decide which solutions to try.

Assume good faith: Everyone is on the same team and everyone wants to make the best product possible. No matter what the art department says, they don't really want to destroy the tech department. They want a flawless, intuitive experience. They just have no idea how to get there. (If they did, they would be the tech department.) Their criticism usually comes from a place of caring, not anger.

Ask them to show you what they mean: Many artists won't have the technical vocabulary needed to express what it is they're trying to get across. Instead of making them explain over and over, let them show you at their desk, on their terms. Go watch them interact with the product and let their actions speak for them.

Don't do all the talking: It's tempting to defend yourself when negative feedback comes in. This usually backfires if it happens in feedback sessions with artistic people. Even if it's a very rational explanation of the limitations of the system, artists will often stop talking altogether, assuming you must be the expert, so their opinion doesn't matter much. Don't volunteer the explanation for why things work the way they look. If the artist asks why, go ahead and explain, but remember you are there to listen, not to lecture.

Be kind: Sometimes the reason for the programming not meeting expectations is heavily impacted by art. For instance, the artists have delivered assets too big for the project, so it slows everything down. When this is the case, and artists are complaining about how slow things are moving, it would be easy to point fingers right back at the art department when this happens. However, it would be more productive to listen carefully to the feedback—then agree with them. Speak in terms of wish lists and specifications. For instance, "You're right. That would be great. We're trying to make it run as smoothly as we can, but that's a lot of big art files it's trying to display all at the same time." Sometimes a comment like this will open the eyes of the art department to just how important the specifications are.

Say thank you: Feedback can be hard to hear. It often feels like a long list of inadequacies and personal attacks. Regardless of how it's delivered, say thank you—sincerely—to the person who provides the feedback. You want to hear about problems before the product is released to the public. You want to know how you can improve your collaboration and your craft. You want friends and colleagues to push you to be better. So even if it feels painful and awkward at the time, be sure to thank the person with fresh eyes who took the time to help you evaluate how the tech is working.

6 Giving It Back

Communication Is a Constant Looping Cycle

Receiving feedback is only the first half of what needs to be a complete loop. To have a clean communication line there needs to be one more step, something the military calls back briefing. This involves responding to what you just heard by explaining back what you just understood. It's most effective when you use your own words instead of just parroting or copy/pasting the original feedback. In this way, the person who provided feedback can gauge how well they were able to communicate their ideas to you.

Sometimes this takes more than one conversation. You confirm your understanding of the feedback immediately after receiving it. Following up again later, to show what specific plans are being made to implement changes, can once again correct any misunderstandings before the change gets out of the planning phase. It also helps to manage expectations. If the original feedback included 10 things that weren't quite right, and you can only address six of them with the current schedule and resources, addressing and explaining these limitations can focus attention on the positives instead of the negatives, even though you're still in the planning phases. "We looked into it, but due to schedule limitations, we're just not going to be able to address these four items. However, these six are going to be addressed in this way ...." This provides closure for the person providing feedback and shows that you genuinely heard what the feedback was—their opinion counted.

And if you focus your backbrief on the things you can change, rather than those you can't, there is less time or energy spent on second-guessing your decisions. Campaigning for a pet change usually only happens when the person giving the feedback is convinced that they haven't been heard or understood, because from their point of view, if you understand why they thought this was important, you would think it was important too.

Try not to be accusatory or defensive. Stay professional and matter-of-fact. Here are some phrases to try:

- What I got from the feedback session was ....

- I heard that there was a problem with ....

- When I took a long look at the feedback, I saw ....

- In the feedback session, I heard ....

A good rule of thumb is to try to avoid using the word "you" because this isn't about the other person at all, really. This is about the effect their words had and the images their words conjured up. Focus on saying "I heard" or "I saw" or "I learned." That way you're not accidentally sounding petty or accusing, as you can if you say, "You told me this ...." or "You said I should make this change."

Feedback should be a constant, looping cycle with the product moving in a spiral upward, constantly improving as the give-and-take of the feedback loop makes it better and better.

7 Professional Courtesy

How to Treat Each Other Well at Work

Sometimes programming is such a rush, it's hard to believe people pay you to have so much fun. Seeing your ideas turn into reality just by using the right words can be amazing. Then there are days when everything is broken, nothing makes sense, and everybody is looking at you for a fix. That's when you show you're a pro and not an amateur. You get the job done, even when it's not fun.

When you work on a team, you also have to make accommodations for teammates who are different from you—whether it's listening to your music with headphones instead of turning the speakers up to 11, or keeping the piles of papers on your desk from invading someone else's workspace—at the heart of it all, being professional means making sure your teammates can work as comfortably as you can. Everybody makes some concessions, and at the end of the day, everybody is productive.

Not distracting your coworkers includes everything from dressing appropriately, keeping body odor under control, and being aware if your food or personal belongings are bothering others.

Beyond these essentials, there are a few more things that can help you work better with artists.

Lunch Topic

Ask artists if they think about their work as an algorithm—you may need to explain what you mean by that. Find out how they make decisions about what to do next, and what it feels like to get feedback before they're ready.

Clear guidelines and specifications: Don't assume the artists already know what you will need. Sure, if they are experienced artists they will have a pretty good idea of what the specifications will be, but they still need to hear it from you—all of it. Whether its aspect ratios, pixel shapes, polly counts, or file sizes, providing more information is better than leaving things off because you think they already know. Whatever technological boundaries affect the art, or are affected by the art, make sure the artists know about them.

Hold them to these standards, too. Don't make things work if they aren't following the technical specifications. Reject it and let them know exactly why it's not going to work—even if these guidelines and requirements won't break things, but they will make things run more smoothly. Artists are capable of rising to the challenge to make their art function inside the programming; it's just more difficult and time consuming sometimes. If they have the restrictions clearly communicated and enforced from the beginning of the project, they will know what is expected of them and can provide what's needed. If they don't know, they will push all the boundaries just to see if they can get away with it. Not because they are trying to break things or cause problems. Just because being creative often means trying new or unusual things.

Clear direction: Artists don't work well when they don't understand what success looks like. They need to be told when they are doing things right, just as much as they need to be told when they are not doing well. In art, the solutions are not binary good/bad or working/broken. Art is analog. Sometimes it's hard to know when you've moved past the midpoint on the continuum from "art doesn't work" to "art works well." The programmers are not usually on the front lines of giving artists clear direction, but you certainly play a part in the process, and sometimes letting them know when they've produced good work can greatly improve the relationship between art and tech.

Reference art: Communicating with artists about their work can be difficult. Two people often describe exactly the same piece of art very differently, even when that art has already been created. So using words to discuss visuals before those visuals exist is understandably difficult. This difficulty can be ameliorated by using similar art, drawing pictures, and providing examples of what you mean.

Communicate about changes, even if the artist doesn't need to make the change: On a large project, it can be easy to silo communication. And it's true, not everybody needs to know about every little change. But everybody does need to know about every big change, even if you don't see how it relates to their job, or it doesn't in any way change the specifications of what they need to do.

There are, however, intangibles. An artist might do something slightly differently if they know about a major change to the overall plan. Even if it won't change the file size or resolution of their assets, they can make the overall project better, smoother, and more cohesive if they are kept in the loop.

And beyond that, it's easy for artists to feel overlooked and underappreciated. On tech-heavy projects, they know that the end goal couldn't be completed without programmers, but art is icing on the cake. The product can still work and achieve its goals, even if it doesn't include their art. The minimum viable product usually doesn't include art. So they are more aware and sensitive about being included on the team. Even if it's not a change that affects them directly, as full team members, they still need to be made aware of the current state of the project.

Don't over-promise: Programmers know how to dream big and plan big. But when talking to artists, make sure you're talking in terms that take into account the very real limitations on every group project. Artists usually

Lunch Topic

Ask artists what they know about how a computer works. If that question is too broad, narrow it down to talking about how touch screens work, or how a program goes from being words on a screen to being a functioning app. Ask them what technology they are most excited to see next, and how long they think it will be before that technology is widely available. These topics can give you a good sense of how different their understanding of technology is.

don't have a good general concept of when you're talking in wishful terms, and when you're talking about real plans. Since most artists don't have a solid understanding of programming, much of what programmers—and technology in general—are capable of doing today seems like straight up magic. So when you tell them you can do something—they believe it. They can't tell when you're talking about "feasible with modern technology" versus "realistically possible within the bounds of the current project." This isn't to say you should never dream big when you're around an artist. Just make sure you tell them that's what you're doing when you do it.

8 Danger Signs

Warning Flags That Communication Is Breaking Down

Your relationship with the art department may not be at the top of your list of things to worry about. It's easy to think as long as things are moving along okay, there's really nothing to fix. The problem is that artists tend to let things fester. Many times they bury their problems and avoid talking about them to people they think won't understand them.

So, there are times when a bad situation gets worse because communication is falling apart but in nonobvious ways. This section sheds light on a few behaviors that range from minorly troublesome to outright annoying. They can sometimes be precursors to worse situations, but often aren't appreciated for the warning signs they are.

This section also provides some suggestions for how to reengage with artists in this situation, which can avoid bigger problems later on.

When the Artists Stop Trying to Talk About Their Art

What it looks like: This is often the first sign that something has gone sour for the artists. It's a generalization, and of course there are always exceptions to the rule, but for the most part artists are eager to talk about their work. They want to talk about what's going well, what's not going well, what's standing in the way of doing better. They want to talk about the philosophy and story behind their creations. If artists are reluctant to talk about their art, or are brief and abrupt when asked about it, there's almost certainly something wrong.

Case Study

Anonymous

Artists at one company were once bitten, twice shy about talking to the programmers ... so when models in the game started showing up rotated off by 90 degrees (programmer bug) they just started silently reexporting everything out to compensate.

Which didn't go over well later when the bug eventually got fixed.

What to do about it: Get them to talk about what's blocking their efforts. And it may seem counterintuitive, but they may be reluctant to talk about it if they think the problem has something to do with you.

Artists tend to try very hard to fix things themselves. They will often bend over backwards making accommodations for other people without even mentioning they are doing it for fear of being seen as a burden, even if the problem would be easily solved by a small change in another department. They do genuinely appreciate help, though, they just don't want to ask for it or look weak.

So to fix this situation, do everything you can to open communication lines. If an artist is reluctant to talk about their art, it usually means that's exactly what needs to happen most. Get them out of the office in small, nonthreatening groups and ask them how things are going with the project. If they just say, "Fine," change the topic. Come back to it after you have established rapport. Use some of the "Lunch Topics" in this book. First get them talking about anything, then ask them what's frustrating them most about the project.

And most importantly—listen. Don't try to problem-solve right away. Ask more clarifying questions and show that you're genuinely interested, and to be sure you know what the problem is before you try to solve it. Then ask if they would like to brainstorm solutions to the problem. Together, you're likely to find answers that can get things flowing smoothly for the artists again. You might need to be the first one to suggest that a different department—even your own—could do something to help. It's possible your art department won't be shy about outlining ways other people can help them, but if that's the case, you've got a highly developed art team there.

When the Artists Deliver Work That Meets Technical Specs but Doesn't Look Good

What it looks like: Artists start submitting work, calling it "finished" when it's clearly not their best work. This is different from the cases where artists do good work, but then forget to test it in combination with the technology. That's a common mistake many beginning artists make. They are often surprised to see what their artwork looks like in the product, in combination with the tech. That's usually a problem with understanding the pipeline and business processes, not a problem with communication.

The communication problem related to art that doesn't look good is different. This is when art meets all the technical specifications, has been tested with the technology, and just doesn't live up to the promise of the artist's previous work. When an artist is phoning it in, it shows in the work, and that level of demotivation is almost always associated with a communication problem.

What to do about it: Bring up a specific piece of art and ask the artist if they are happy with it. They might dodge the question by saying something like, "It meets specifications" or more frequently, "It's what they asked for." Don't let that go by as the answer. Acknowledge that it satisfies the requirements, but keep pushing—do they like it? Are they happy with it? Usually you can get them to admit that it's not their best work, and then you've got the opening to ask why—what's holding them back? Can anybody help?

Sometimes the answers are beyond your control—short deadlines, conflicting direction, confusing vision. But sometimes the answers reveal ways that the tech department has stepped on toes, overstepped boundaries, or are trying to solve a technical problem with an artistic solution.

So, ask questions. Make sure you aren't making life harder on the artists, and find out if there's anything you can do to help.

When the Artists Deliver Work Late or Incomplete

What it looks like: It's not unusual for an artist to be a bit behind sometimes. Artistic inspiration can be unreliable, and being creative

Lunch Topic

Ask artists two questions: First, what is the slowest part of your process or pipeline? Then, what's the most boring part? A lot of times there are miscommunications about processes that aren't obvious until two different departments truly understand each other's methods. Sometimes a programmer can create a tool very quickly which can save hours on the art process. When that happens, the tech department becomes the artists' heroes.

on demand is hit-and-miss sometimes. But a pattern of constantly turning in every asset late is a bigger issue than an occasionally reluctant muse.

What to do about it: Once again, the solution is to proactively try to open up the lines of communication. Ask open-ended questions, not pointed accusations like, "Why are you always delivering late?" Rather, think about questions that don't sound accusatory. "Is there something holding you guys back?" Or maybe, "Is there something slowing down the pipeline?" The artists are probably afraid that the problem is entirely with them, and they have probably been trying to fix it by themselves. Getting them out of their isolation and feelings of hopelessness can kick-start their productivity. Sometimes just having the conversation and showing them they are important to you as human beings—not just generators of art—can make a big difference for their output.

When Artists Argue More Than They Create

What it looks like: This one seems like a problem of too much communicating, but really it's about procrastinating. Artists are often very passionate people, and sometimes spend more time arguing about design, tech, overall direction, and individuals, rather than sitting down to make art assets. This can be a big problem, since extra time is rarely a luxury these kinds of projects have.

Keep in mind, this warning sign is only valid if the arguments from the art department are getting in the way of productivity. If the conversations are useful and move the project along, this isn't at all a problem.

And the art department can have a very unusual work process, where asset building happens at the same time as talking. So again, don't confuse a lot of productive talking with this warning sign.

You'll know this one when you see it. There will be big meetings, individual bitching sessions, and a lot of nitpicking—but no art.

What to do about it: Get the artists to talk about the real problem, rather than focusing on other problems surrounding it. Many times this is a deeply personal issue—for instance, holding a grudge about their ideas not being taken seriously, or fearing that they aren't good enough artists to provide the assets required. Talking about everything except art often signals a lack of confidence in the artist, and that can be very difficult for anyone to open up about.

The first thing to do is to set aside some time to just listen. Artists in these circumstances often feel they're not being heard—even though other team members might see the artists taking up everyone's time with arguments and complaints. Keep in mind that when someone feels like they've been genuinely heard through, they often stop talking. So, make time to do nothing other than listen to the art department. Ask them clarifying questions and repeat back what they've said, using your own words to show you've been paying attention to them.

When they start to wind down, ask them if all these things they've been talking about have been getting in the way of creating the actual art assets. Express how much you're looking forward to seeing their art, and express your confidence in their ability to do it. It's possible this will be enough. It's also possible when you start saying these things, the artists will be able to open up about what's really getting in the way of art production. Maybe they don't fully understand the vision for the final product—or don't like it, or have confidence in it. Maybe they like the vision, but think they're not the right artists for the job.

Case Study
Squirrel Eiserloh, Lead Programmer

The single most effective improvement to programmer-art communication I have seen was when Ken Harwood at Ritual Entertainment mandated that programmers must get out of their chairs and go sit down next to any artist reporting a tool/pipeline/engine issue, and witness the artist experiencing the issue firsthand at her desk, and let her demonstrate and explain the issue in her own terms while the programmer sat and listened. AMAZING amounts of workflow empathy, cross-departmental trust, and close working relationships were generated.

And so sad how obvious this was in hindsight.

Get them to talk about it—then get them to commit to trying. Point out that others can't see the problems they do without seeing art added into the mix. Maybe it is a weak vision—but others won't be able to see it until they start seeing art. Try to convince them they have some power to change things by providing art assets.

Don't hint or suggest that any of the problems they are complaining about are their fault or being exacerbated by the complaining—even if that's the case. Remember the artists are usually looking to be heard, not necessarily looking for a quick fix.

 Mending Fences

How to Talk about Fixing a Broken Communication Line

Even if communication has completely broken down between the art department and the tech department, there's always a way back. You're all working on the same project, and have the same end goal—to do the best job you can in the time provided. It's always worthwhile to try to improve communications.

Artists who are disconnected from the rest of the developers don't create the best art. So even if you think they can't contribute to technical problem-solving conversations, an improved communication line can make your final product much better and easier for end users. A broken communication line with the art department is a bug. It will lower the quality of your work; everything is intertwined.

So, in the interest of improving your final creation, take the steps to fix this bug. Sure, it's a peopleware bug, but without people the software doesn't get created. Ignoring this problem means shipping with a bug.

Identify the problem: Just as you do with software, the first step in fixing the problem is to identify and define it. Use this book to help pin down what has gone wrong with communication and put a box around it. Identify parts of the communication process which do work, and compare them to the ones that don't. Similarities could mean you're using the wrong tool for the job. Differences could mean you're not using the proven solutions.

Formulate a possible solution: Come up with a plan for changing how you will communicate with the art department. Keep in mind that this is only a guess. Stay open to alternate solutions and ideas. For now, you're only looking at your side of the issue, and focus on solutions where the effort to change is also on your side.

Put it on paper: Put this plan down on paper, maybe in paragraph format, but try it in a flowchart. Artists pick up information in a visual format very quickly. But do whatever it takes to clearly explain both the problem and your potential solution.

Have a meeting: Ask for a meeting with the primary stakeholders— the art lead, producer, tech lead, etc. For this conversation, probably not every artist needs to be in the room. The producer or project manager is the key, however, because a broken (or even slow) communication line can cause deadlines to slip and schedules to stretch out far longer than they really need to be.

Bring an agenda such as this one:

Agenda

Art/Tech miscommunication

- Examples of miscommunication

- Consequences of miscommunication

- Causes of miscommunication

  - Listening?

  - Clear messages?

Solution Brainstorm

- What can art do to improve?

- What can tech do to improve?

Be prepared to let the other side vent a little. Let them suggest solutions. Don't try to dictate what they will do in the future. Ask nicely and be prepared for pushback.

Try this: Think about how you can change your approach. Ultimately, what the art department does is out of your hands and out of your control, so focus on what you can do to improve the situation, even if they don't change at all.

Avoid this: Prescribing specifics for how the art department needs to change their approach will likely be fruitless. While art and tech have things in common (creativity, same project, same goals), the methods they use are vastly different and most people are not well-versed in both of them. Change what you can change—yourselves. And be clear about what you need from the art department—both output and input. But don't try to tell them how to create it. Focus on the ends, not the means. Artists usually have an antiauthoritarian streak in their personalities that reflexively balks when someone else tries to tell them what to do—even if it's a great idea.

Try this: Show them you appreciate them. Artists tend to appreciate gestures. Bring food. Compliment their art. Say the words, "I'm sorry" and mean them.

Avoid this: Programmers often focus on actions and think words are a waste of time. If you realize you have done something wrong, or even just that you have contributed in some way to the problem, you will often take action quickly and fix the malfunctioning process—even if it's a human process and not a computer program. What is often overlooked, however, is the uncomfortable and inefficient step of talking about it. Saying the words "That was my mistake. I'm sorry." Programmers may not care much if those words aren't spoken. They expect their actions will speak louder than words. This works really well with other programmers, but artists need to hear the words. They find this step to be crucial. Artists will wonder whether programmers really understand the problem if they haven't voiced the words—even if they have made the changes.

This isn't because they want to waste your time. Rather, they need to know the motivations and intentions behind the change in behavior. They may see and appreciate your efforts, but they are likely to be very suspicious of them, having to guess at what your intentions are. If the change is motivated by your awareness that something was broken, and now you're trying to fix it—they need to hear it. Otherwise, they will worry that the change is incidental and not in any way permanent. They are likely to fear that the problem has not truly been recognized, and may continue behaving as if the problem still exists when it doesn't. That's because artists tend to focus on intentions and ideas over concrete actions.

Case Study
Mike Sellers, Creative Director

On another project there was a difficult, simmering relationship between the lead artist and lead engineer on a team of about 40 people that took me a little while to unwind. It took lots of meetings, along with some downward pressure from me as their boss. Trying to get them each to understand the needs of the other group, and not play on their fears. I even made them just go take walks around the campus a few times. Eventually, we got it all worked out. The two leads even became strong allies, and things worked incredibly well.

Try this: Take time to tell the artists what they're doing right. Acknowledge that their job is not easy to do, and establish that you know the project would be inferior without their contribution. Sometimes just acknowledging this fact can bring on a flood of communication from the art department. If they are feeling like nobody appreciates their effort, they often clam up and stop trying to problem-solve. And even if it doesn't break a logjam by talking about it, everyone likes to hear they are appreciated. It can generally improve relations even if nothing specific changes.

Avoid this: Other people in the team often characterize art contributions as easy or simple, while at the same time putting enormous pressure on every detail. Don't minimize the effort they put into the project, and try to avoid saying things like, "This is just an art bug" or "This won't take long, it's just an art task." The word "just" makes it seem like the task is unimportant or easy, when the artist is the one who has to do the work and knows how hard or easy it is.

Eating Crow

How to Apologize and Make Friends if Something Goes Wrong

Nobody likes apologizing, but sometimes it's the right thing to do. If you discover that part of the communication breakdown has been exacerbated by something the tech department has done or said, take responsibility for it. Even if nobody else has realized this is where the problem started, they will appreciate knowing that you are working on a fix for the problem.

There are some key parts of a real apology that often get skipped in our rush to get out of an awkward conversation. Don't skip them. Each of these steps builds on each other and together they form a genuine apology that can keep awkward conversations from becoming the norm.

Say you are sorry. Do not say you are sorry they are offended or sad: Say you are sorry for what you have done that contributed to them feeling that way. Their feelings are out of your control. Sure, you may be sorry they are feeling excluded from important conversations, or you may be sorry they are angry. That's not part of an apology, though. That's just a statement of your feelings about their feelings. Say you are sorry for what you did—you've been skipping meetings they called, or you have been unclear in some of your specifications. Whatever it is you have discovered is at the heart of the problem on your end. Tell them you are sorry for what you did—not what they did. Speak about your regret, not about them.

Show you understand how they are feeling: This is about acknowledging how your actions affected someone else. This isn't where you say you are sorry. Instead focus on how to acknowledge their frustration, anger, etc. "When we did that, it meant you all had a ton of new work to do, and we didn't take that into account." Whatever emotion you have seen from them, acknowledge it.

Be clear that you made a mistake. Take responsibility for it: Say what it was you did—whether it's making unilateral decisions without first consulting them, or not providing enough explanation for how the systems work. Even assuming something was a common knowledge, and not taking the time to follow up on it can be a mistake. You don't need to say you are a bad person, just own the thing you did.

Share your plan for moving forward in a new way: This is how you show that things will be different from here on out. This can't be vague or skipped over. Explain how you will behave from now on, and ask if this will help. Welcome their feedback if they have any. This part of the apology goes best if it becomes a conversation, not just a one-sided speech. Explain your plan and get their acknowledgment that it will help—or at least their willingness to try it and see if it helps.

Promise to uphold your part of this new way of behaving: After hashing out a new plan, or getting confirmation that the plan you brought to the table is a good one for both sides, take the final step to promise that you will do your part to make this plan a reality.

• • • • • • • • • • • • • • • • • • • •
Lunch Topic

Share stories about the worst/funniest/most aggravating bugs you've ever fixed. Bonus points for admitting you made the mistake in the first place. Try to explain how the problem slipped through the cracks, how it was found, and what it took to fix it. Do all of this in terms the artists understand. Don't technobabble.

Sharing these embarrassing moments can help others see you as human, approachable and honest. They are more likely to forgive quickly when something goes wrong in the future, and provides a vocabulary and context for talking about problems.
• • • • • • • • • • • • • • • • • • • •

Commit to following through on your side of the plan. And that's it, you're done with your apology.

While going through the mechanics listed above is important to building a healthy relationship with the art department, keep in mind that the artist mind tends to appreciate material gestures. Say the words and follow up, but it might not hurt to come to the apology meeting bearing donuts. Take them out to lunch—you pay for it— one day soon after. Or go out for drinks or some other activity in an evening where the tech department foots the bill for the artists. These kinds of gestures mean a lot to them.

(1) Artist Dictionary

Disambiguating Words Artists Use

Artists and programmers each have their own lingo. When they are in groups made up of people like themselves, the jargon can be so thick nobody on the outside can possibly follow what they're saying. This dictionary is not about that language. Artists learn it over years of training, and it works really well to communicate clearly with other people who have been trained in the same way.

This dictionary is different. It focuses on words that artists and programmers use when they are talking to people who don't already know their lingo. They drop the jargon and use normal words—or at least normal-sounding words. The words are normal enough that nobody stops to ask what they really mean by that. Everyone thinks they already understand. So, misunderstandings multiply one word at a time, and somehow the miscommunication can grow exponentially.

These words aren't especially complicated. Many of them are common English words with lots of nuance and multiple definitions. We focus here on what artists usually mean when they say these words, and how it differs from what programmers might expect when they hear those words.

3D—adjective or noun

What artists may say: *"We can't do this in 3D."*

What artists usually mean: Using a program to build virtual sculptures of every element, animating them in complex, intricate simulations. Alternately, stereoscopic cameras and filters will be required to simulate depth and dimension.

What artists usually don't mean: Everything will look like paper cutouts with no depth. Artists have used techniques like perspective and shading for centuries to make two-dimensional (2D) art look like it is three-dimensional (3D). There are even techniques artists can use in two-dimension to make things look impossibly 3D. Just think of MC Escher's staircase that folds back into itself. However, the term 3D has a very specific meaning.

Bright—adjective

What artists may say: *"I need to make that brighter."*

What artists usually mean: This can be a very ambiguous word. Making something brighter (or making it less bright) could involve anything from adjusting textures to changing the saturation on the color. It doesn't always mean they will be changing the lighting. There are many ways of solving this problem, and figuring out the best way to do it is usually best left to the individual artist on the specific project. What has worked in the past may not work this time.

What artists usually don't mean: I will adjust the lighting.

Color Wheel—noun

What artists may say: *"Let me look at a color wheel for a while."*

What artists usually mean: Colors are formally organized into a wheel with the colors moving in rainbow order around in a circle. Red- > Orange- > Yellow- > Green- > Blue- > Violet and the violet is up against red again on the other side. This organizational method displays the relationships between colors and explains how they will be perceived when shown together.

What artists sometimes don't mean: The color picker circle where the colors blend into each other and help show a variety of hues to be selected by the user.

Cool—adjective

What artists may say: *"This fire is too cool. It's a problem."*

What artists usually mean: Colors are formally organized into a wheel with the colors moving in rainbow order around in a circle. The green/blue/violet side of the color wheel is called the "cool" side of the color wheel. Red/orange/yellow are the "warm" side. Color temperature is also used to describe the relative position of different hues of the same color. For example, a blue located closer to the green side of the color wheel is "cooler" than a blue located closer to the violet side. One would be a "cool blue," and the other a "warm blue," even though all blues fall on the "cool" side of the color wheel.

What artists sometimes don't mean: This is very trendy.

Contrast—noun

What artists may say: *"I need to add more contrast here."*

What artists usually mean: Elements in the piece need a bigger difference in their light/dark color palette or their warm/cool color palette.

What artists usually don't mean: I will add more black outlines.

Depth—noun

What artists may say: *"These stairs need more depth."*

What artists usually mean: Artists refer to "deep colors," as those that have more dark brown or black added. They may also talk about bit depth and "deep color" as the technology of high-end graphics stations.

What artists usually don't mean: Doesn't refer only to physical depth of an object, either modeled or implied through perspective.

Dithering—noun

What artists may say: *"I don't like the dithering on this."*

What artists usually mean: Dithering is a method of making images with just a few colors look more realistic, without color banding. You can think of it as the slightly speckled look of low-quality digital images, though it's a complex mathematical method of breaking up unwanted patterns.

What artists usually don't mean: Being indecisive or argumentative.

Easy—adjective or adverb

What artists may say: *"That will be easy."*

What artists usually mean: This will come together relatively quickly and with little effort.

What they don't mean: *"That will be done."* An artist agreeing that something is easy does not mean that artist has agreed to do the thing being discussed. They have only commented on the hypothetical difficulty.

Feature—adjective, noun, verb

What artists may say: *"This is a feature piece."*

What artists usually mean: The word "feature" can be used in several different ways, but artists often think of it in terms of "showing off" or "bringing attention to" one particular element of the whole. A single feature piece might be made with special attention and detail to draw the eye. It often means the artist worked harder or longer on this than on other art assets.

What artists usually don't mean: The various functions of the overall product.

Fluid—adjective

What artists may say: *"We'd like to have water sloshing against that edge."*

"We'd like to use some fluid dynamics for the particles of dust in the air."

"Everything needs to be very fluid and organic."

What artists usually mean: Artist want particles to move in a realistic way when the player interacts with them. This doesn't necessarily mean it needs to be complicated mathematics. This could also simply refer to smooth and curvy lines instead of sharp angles and straight lines. Artists think in visuals, not processes.

What artists usually don't mean: This won't work unless we figure out how to simulate fluid dynamics to a high degree of fidelity in real time.

Finished—verb

What artists may say: *"I'm not finished yet."*
"I'll get to that when I'm finished here."

What artists usually mean: Artists never feel finished. Remember that the tools they use to get their concepts out of their head and into the real world are subjective. The image on screen or paper rarely looks exactly the way they imagined it, though to others it may look spectacular and complete. Artists are always comparing the image in front of them with the one they have imagined, and the real one never quite matches up. So, they are hesitant to describe something as "finished" though they may agree that something is "good enough." There's always potential for the asset to be better or more refined.

What artists usually don't mean: They don't intend to hold things back just to be obstinate. They are often hesitant to show a work-in-progress, just as anyone would be.

Hot—adjective

What artists may say: *"This corner is too hot."*

What artists usually mean: The word "hot" is sometimes used to refer to the brightness or intensity of colors.

What artists usually don't mean: "This corner is very trendy and awesome."

Hue—noun

What artists may say: *"The hue of this sand looks off, it looks more like a warmer beach sand than the sand you would find in a rock quarry."*

What artists usually mean: Many people think of "hue" as meaning the same thing as "color." However, an artist thinks of color as a combination of hue, value, and saturation. The hue is the pure color, where it falls on the color wheel. The value and saturation can be changed while the hue remains the same. The overall effect is quite different, whether you change the hue, the saturation, or the value.

What artists usually don't mean: Simply color—although it's close enough to be synonymous most of the time.

Lighting—noun or verb

What artists may say: *"No, I can't change the lighting."*

What artists usually mean: Lighting can be a complicated subject in technical projects, and it's not always something artists have direct control over. They may be able to control how their asset looks when it's lit, but they don't always have control of the lighting themselves. Note that they may be able to make something brighter without changing the lighting. Lighting gets particularly complicated on 3D-rendered art.

What artists usually don't mean: I don't like your suggestion, so I'm going to play dumb.

Midnight—noun

What artists may say: *"This automated build didn't run at the right time."*

What artists usually mean: Artists think of midnight as the last minute of a day, not the first. It's sometimes context-dependent, but the vast majority of the time, artists expect "Midnight on Thursday" to come right after Thursday 11:59 p.m. Those originally from the United States are also less familiar with a 24-hour clock. Saying something is set to begin at 9:00 could have two meanings to an artist (AM or PM).

What artists usually don't mean: They don't mean to be stubborn about this. It's just what they're used to.

Model—noun or verb

What artists may say: *"I'll need time to model this."*

What artists usually mean: Creating a 3D art asset using a program specifically created for that purpose. Those models may then be exported for use in other applications.

What artists usually don't mean: Does not mean "simulate" or building something physical.

Modular—adjective

What artists may say: *"We can make some modular art."*

What artists usually mean: Puzzle pieces that fit seamlessly together.

What artists usually don't mean: Modular art can't be used in unlimited ways. Many times two specific pieces are intended to fit together in particular arrangements. Other arrangements or stretching the art in ways it wasn't designed to work with can often upset the artists, even if it was intended to be an asset that is reusable and somewhat flexible. For instance, changing aspect ratios can be problematic.

Network—verb

What artists may say: *"Let's network this problem."*

What artists usually mean: This word is used to refer to talking to people to ask for help, ideas, or opinions as often—or more often—than it means computers talking to computers.

What artists sometimes don't mean: Connecting computers over a network.

Numbers—noun

What artists may say: *"Your numbered list makes no sense."*

What artists usually mean: Artists begin with one when they count. They are often confused or think programmers are joking when they start counting with zero. They are prone to skipping the first step of something if it is listed as item zero.

What artists usually don't mean: They don't mean to be obnoxious about this. It's just how they think.

Paint—verb

What artists may say: *"No, I can't just paint that red."*

What artists usually mean: Paint is a specific tool artists use, usually in nondigital circumstances. Some tools simulate paint, but it's a fairly complex process.

What artists usually don't mean: To artists, this doesn't just mean "change an item's color."

Perspective—noun

What artists may say: *"We need to give this some perspective."*

What artists usually mean: Perspective can be a complicated topic. Essentially, things that are faraway look smaller to the human eye than things that are up close. This is how paintings and other art displayed on a flat surface manages to give the impression that there is a background and a foreground without actually being a 3D-rigged model. There are even different kinds of perspectives—for instance, two-point, three-point, fisheye, and forced. In video games, perspective is sometimes used to refer to the position of the camera.

What artists usually don't mean: Just the viewing angle alone. There's a lot more to it than that.

Repurpose—verb

What artists may say: *"Yes, you can repurpose that texture."*

What artists usually mean: Use an asset in a different way than it was originally intended—but don't change the art itself by stretching or resizing. Put it in a different context, turn it upside down, use it on the top instead of the bottom, etc. For instance, a single rock can be repurposed multiple times if it is created with that intent. Turning it over, setting it up at different angles, or piling them together can make one asset seem like a dozen.

What artists usually don't mean: Stretching, warping, or resizing the art in the new context so it no longer looks the way they intend it to look. This can make an artist very grumpy.

Resize—verb

What artists may say: *"Yes, I can resize that piece."*

What artists usually mean: A new version of the asset will be created at the correct aspect ratio and resolution.

What artists usually don't mean: The asset will be enlarged or reduced without taking into account how that will affect it at the level of the pixels.

Shrink—verb

What artists may say: *"Please don't shrink this down."*

What artists usually mean: It's often possible to squeeze an art asset down into a size smaller than it was originally created. To more technical people, this often seems like a good idea and not a big deal. However, it will often end up looking sufficiently different that artists will notice, and not like the effect.

What artists usually don't mean: Art assets are totally inflexible. Artists can make art somewhat flexible, but they need to do it in special ways. Communicate with them in detail if this is something you want to do.

Stretch—verb

What artists may say: *"Please don't stretch my art."*

What artists usually mean: No matter how the art is used, don't change the aspect ratio of assets. The interpolation algorithms in the video drivers distort stretched assets in ways programmers aren't trained to notice, but can be very distracting under some circumstances. It's more efficient to avoid stretching art, using multiple similar assets if necessary, rather than do exhaustive scenario testing.

What artists usually don't mean: Art can never be made to change shape or move dynamically.

Tile—verb

What artists may say: *"I can make that tile across the back."*

What artists usually mean: They can create a small piece, usually square, that replicates across a field, being copied over and over, set right next to each version of itself. The intent is usually to make the transition seamless.

What artists usually don't mean: They will make it look like bathroom tile.

Value—noun

What artists may say: *"What's the value of that box?"*

What artists usually mean: Artists think of the word value as it relates to the lightness or darkness of a color. Different hues can have the same value—the same amount of dark or light added—and then they look pretty much the same if they are rendered in grayscale. The word "value" is used a lot in talking about color theory, though it tends to be used more in color theory as it relates to physical pigments (like paint on canvas) as opposed to the interactions of colored light (like on a computer screen).

What artists usually don't mean: The HTML RGB numbers.

Warm—adjective

What artists may say: *"We need to warm up this lighting a bit."*

What artists usually mean: Colors are formally organized into a wheel with the colors moving in rainbow order around in a circle. Red/orange/yellow are the "warm" side of the color wheel. Green/blue/violet are the "cool" side. Color temperature is also used to describe the relative position of different hues of the same color. For example, a red located closer to the violet side of the color wheel is "cooler" than a red located closer to the orange side. One would be a "cool red," and the other a "warm red," even though all reds fall on the "warm" side of the color wheel.

What artists usually don't mean: Artists usually aren't talking about intensity when they say something is too warm. If they are referring to intensity, they may say it is too hot.

Zero—noun

What artists may say: *"We have to start over at zero."*

What artists usually mean: Artists begin with one when they count. They are often confused or think programmers are joking when they start counting with zero. They are prone to skipping the first step of something if it is listed as item zero. For them, zero literally means nothing.

What artists usually don't mean: "We know what we need to do first."

Artists Index

Talking to Artists / Talking to
Programmers

How to Get Programmers and Artists Communicating

Talking to Artists / Talking to
Programmers
How to Get Programmers and Artists Communicating

Wendy Despain

CRC Press
Taylor & Francis Group
Boca Raton   London   New York

CRC Press is an imprint of the
Taylor & Francis Group, an **informa** business

AN A K PETERS BOOK

CRC Press
Taylor & Francis Group
6000 Broken Sound Parkway NW, Suite 300
Boca Raton, FL 33487-2742

Printed on acid-free paper
Version Date: 20161107

International Standard Book Number-13: 978-1-4987-0073-3 (Paperback)

Library of Congress Cataloging-in-Publication Data

Names: Despain, Wendy, author.
Title: Talking to artists, talking to programmers : how to get programmers and artists communicating / by Wendy Despain.
Description: Boca Raton, FL : CRC Press, Taylor & Francis Group, 2016. | Includes bibliographical references and index.
Identifiers: LCCN 2016030818| ISBN 9781498700733 (pbk. : alk. paper) | ISBN 9781315381626 (ebook : alk. paper)
Subjects: LCSH: Interpersonal communication. | Intergroup relations. | Artists--Professional relationships. | Computer programmers--Professional relationships. | Video games industry--Social aspects.
Classification: LCC HM1166 .D48 2016 | DDC 302.3--dc23
LC record available at https://lccn.loc.gov/2016030818

Visit the Taylor & Francis Web site at
http://www.taylorandfrancis.com

and the CRC Press Web site at
http://www.crcpress.com

Contents

Contents

Preface: Talking to Programmers

A rtists and programmers often work together on complex projects in stressful environments and things don't always go smoothly. Miscommunication and misunderstandings are common as these two disciplines often use the same words to mean different things when they talk to each other. Unintentional slights can turn into long-held grudges and productivity grinds to a crawl.

This book can help anyone who wants to improve communication with artists and programmers. It's set up like a foreign language dictionary, so it addresses the cultural norms, attitudes and customs surrounding the words each group uses, so you'll know not just what the words in the glossary mean, you'll know why they're used that way and how to get communication flowing again.

It addresses common reasons for communication problems between these two groups and provides specific suggestions for solutions. The unusual format allows for each side to be given equal weight—learn how to talk to artists starting on one side of this book, turn it over and learn how to talk to programmers. The whole book stresses the things artists and programmers have in common.

Focused primarily on video game developers, it also applies to other fields where tech and art have to work together, including web developers and teams building mobile apps. This book can help anyone who wants to communicate better with programmers or artists.

Acknowledgments

I would like to thank all the people who encouraged me to write this book, especially Aerin Artessa, the artist who urged me to finish as soon as possible. I would also like to thank all those—both artists and programmers—who reviewed the material and provided case studies. Especially when you pointed out the places where I was sounding mean instead of blunt. I deeply appreciate your honesty and hope I have rectified the problems. There are also many students, who will remain anonymous, who helped me spot patterns and clarify solutions as we worked through these situations on their teams. I also appreciate all the people who made the clever cover on the book everything it is—from the editorial team who believed in my vision to Mario Rodriguez who helped me practice what I am preaching. And finally, I would like to thank Giles Schildt, former Director of Game Development for SJ Games, who reviewed the manuscript thoroughly for me and made excellent suggestions.

Author

Wendy Despain is a videogame writer and narrative designer with more than a decade of experience spearheading digital media projects. She has worked with teams around the world as a team leader, designer and consultant on console and PC games, mobile apps, online experiences, alternate reality games (ARG), and augmented reality. Some of her credits include an ARG for *Gene Roddenberry's Andromeda*, *Jetset Secrets* on Facebook, and *Fusion Fall* from Cartoon Network. She is currently teaching team building and production strategies at SMU Guildhall in Plano, TX. Her other books include *Professional Techniques for Videogame Writing* (AK Peters/CRC Press, 2008), *Writing For Videogame Genres: From FPS to RPG* (AK Peters/CRC Press, 2009), and *100 Principles of Game Design* (New Riders, 2012).

① Making Sense

Framing the Conversation

Working as an artist in a highly technical project can feel like you've stumbled into an alternate universe where people think strings of code are "elegant" and eight colors are more than enough for every situation. There's little to no appreciation, sometimes, for a well-balanced use of emptiness, or the motion of a viewer's eye through the piece.

It can be lonely and strange. Programmers sometimes come across as arrogant, self-centered, and dour. They have a hard time looking at situations from anyone else's point of view, and have little appreciation for how hard artists work.

But if you look beneath the surface you may find you have more in common with them than you ever believed. At the root of most of the mystifying behavior and uncomfortable conversation is a fundamental miscommunication. They simply don't know how to talk to people who are not technically inclined. And compounding the problem is a frustrating language quirk.

There are common words in both Tech and Art domains, but they're used in very different ways. It's similar to the regional differences in everyday conversations. Ask two English speakers—one from England and one from America—what the word "vest" means,

and you'll get two completely different answers (Worn over a shirt? Or under a shirt?). That's why this book is set up like a foreign language dictionary.

You can use it to find out more about how programmers might be using words in ways that may be slightly—or completely—different from how you do. You can also use it to help explain to them how you use the words. There's a dictionary for them, too.

But even if they're not interested in fixing a communication problem (they may not be aware of how they're contributing to it), you can still use this book to find out how you can change the way you talk so that they understand. Or find out what they mean when they start sending feedback to you in their native language.

Sometimes trying to communicate with the tech side of a complex project seems to stir up more trouble than it's worth. But to have a really high-quality product, everyone has to be moving in the same direction, and valuable time can be lost if you're depending on one or two individuals to shuttle messages back and forth from the art department to the Tech department.

But if you can learn to talk to each other, you can even find ways to collaborate and take the project from "quality" to "fantastic."

And there's more to this book than just a dictionary. If you're going to learn how to communicate clearly in another culture, you have to learn about that culture, not just the vocabulary. That's why we have sections explaining how programmers think and how to approach them.

How to Use This Book

This book is divided up into sections and subsections. The two main sections are mirror images of each other. The Art side and the Tech side both have the same chapter names with the same goals—to teach artists how to speak tech, and techies how to speak art.

Dictionary: Each side of this book includes a dictionary of commonly confused terms. The Art side explains what these terms mean to an artist, and the Tech side explains what these terms mean to a techie. Some suggestions on how to use the dictionary are

- If someone from the tech team uses a word in a meeting that you're not quite sure about, look it up in the dictionary.

- Read through page by page to familiarize yourself with the vocabulary so that you can use them correctly when talking to programmers.

- If you are tempted to use a specific word when providing feedback to programmers, look it up on both sides of the dictionary before using it. Share the definitions with the person you're going to be talking to so you can start out on the same page.

Lunch topics: Throughout this book, there are sidebars that pull out important concepts which can help build bridges across the divide between Art and Tech. They provide suggestions for how to bring up the topic, how to get people talking and onto the same page. These topics don't have to happen over lunch, although food can be a great social lubricant. Bring them up as everyone is standing around the Friday donuts, or when you go out for drinks after a major milestone.

• • • • • • • • • • • • • • • •
Lunch Topic
Pick a word from the programmer's dictionary and ask programmers about how they use the word personally, or how it applies specifically on your project.
• • • • • • • • • • • • • • • •

But if you make it an agenda item for a staff meeting, assuming you've got that kind of pull, be careful. These topics can be sensitive and emotional sometimes, and best covered in a casual, nonthreatening environment where people don't feel like they have to defend themselves.

Case studies: Throughout this book are specific, real-world examples of communication breaking down between the Art department and the Tech department. Most of them are verbatim as they were told to me. Some of them have been edited slightly for clarity, while others have had identifying features changed. This isn't about placing blame or shaming. It's about learning from each other and sharing best practices.

Problem-surf: Consider what specific problems your team may be facing right now, and skim through this book looking at subheads and bolded words that relate to your problem. Reading just those sections can help a lot, although the rest of this book can put things

in context and fix the underlying issues. The dictionary section can be a fun place to start.

Cover to cover: While this is the traditional way to read a book, it won't quite work this time. If you haven't tried to read the back cover yet ... give it a try now. You'll find there isn't one. To read this book fully, you'll have to pick a side and read to the middle, then turn it over and read to the middle again.

As an artist, you'll probably find the "Talking to Programmers" side of this book to be the most useful. You probably already know quite a bit about how to talk to other artists. If you want to read that side of this book, you may gain some insights into how programmers see you. This might open doors of communication and help solve problems, just because you've learned more about how you are perceived. The same territory is covered on both sides. So if you're curious about the advice being given to programmers about how to communicate with you—by all means, dive in to that side of this book.

Study guide: This book can be used in a semiformal or formal learning environment as well. Use it as a textbook in staff training meetings with assigned readings. Lunch topics become group discussion topics.

Gift: Drop it on the desk of the lead programmer and tell them you would like to know what they think about it. Try not to just do this as a drive-by thing. Be genuine. Use this book as a gift to help break the ice.

No matter how you use this book, open your mouth and start talking. Just like any foreign language, practice with native speakers is essential in order to become truly fluent. Admit you're learning, and this is all new to you and you'll be surprised how willing programmers will be to meet you in the middle for a conversation.

# Working Together

Common Problems and Pitfalls, Plus Solutions

The most important thing to remember is that you aren't alone. Programmers and artists have been clashing on projects for decades. It's common and normal if you find yourself in any of the following situations. Don't blame yourself for it, and don't beat yourself up about it. These problems are intrinsic in the combination of art and technology. Below is a list of some common difficulties.

If any of them look familiar, don't agonize over it. Instead of wondering why you didn't instinctively solve a problem others have grappled with for a long time, think of it as a challenge. Maybe think of it like a dense jungle that others have tried to travel through, but nobody has tamed. These are clues and suggestions left by previous explorers as advice to those who come after them.

Hopefully you'll find a few scenarios described here that sound familiar. First is a description of the problem, so you can recognize it when you encounter it on your adventures. It includes warning signs, key features of the problem, and some explanation of how it arises. Then there are specific suggestions for handling these issues, ideas for navigating the dangerous area ahead.

Vague Requirements

What it looks like: Programmers can sometimes provide requirements and directions that are an infuriating combination of the specific and vague. They can give you specific dimensions, resolution, and polygon counts—a whole load of numbers—and then somehow forget to tell you what it is they're expecting to see in those dimensions. A ghost? A pirate? A drop-down menu? But then if you give it your best guess, more often than not they're angry with you for producing the "wrong" thing (though they never told you what the "right" thing would be).

Case Study

Squirrel Eiserloh, Lead Programmer

A set of technical jargon-filled programmer bullet-point mandates about how big to make your textures (powers of two, min/max sizes, min/max aspect ratios etc.) led one confused artist to create a 1024 × 1024 RGBA skin for an arrow ... which was 50% of our video ram budget at the time (1998).

What to do about it: This is a two-step process. First, thank them for whatever clear requirements you were given. Point out specific parts of the requirements that are helpful. Make sure the tech department knows you appreciate what they gave you, and that you're going to follow whatever direction they did give you. Even though you were going to do that from the start, programmers need to hear the reassurances from you before you move on to the next step.

If you skip over step one, the programmers will be afraid that you didn't read the requirements they gave you, and they can get stuck on reiterating the points you've already incorporated into your plans. They will fear that you are taking their efforts for granted.

The second step is to ask specific questions before you start working. Try saying back to them what it is you heard them say, but in your own words. This will give them a chance to identify any areas they didn't communicate clearly. When you have enough information to start working, make a few assets using the requirements as you understand them. Check those assets with the programming department to make sure it's what they need. Don't just show them on a printout or screen. Send them the file and ask them to integrate it into the system as a test.

If possible, watch while they do this and have a conversation with the programmer who is doing the integration. Make sure you understand how the pieces fit together. If your pipeline involves having artists do the integration, ask a programmer to watch while you test the pipeline with these assets. They can learn a lot about what specifications you need to know during that process.

Shifting Pipelines or Needlessly Complex Pipelines

What it looks like: Every few weeks someone from the tech department is sent over to tell the artists they need to be doing things differently—different aspect ratios, different programs for preparing the art for final use, different places on the network, and different file types. Sure, these kinds of things do evolve over the course of a project, and sometimes refining the process can clear up some serious headaches. But if the landscape is constantly changing, and art made before the change has to be updated every time, you'll end up with a huge backlog you can never recover from.

The tech team doesn't always take into consideration how these kinds of decisions will impact your workload.

What to do about it: Make sure you understand why any change is happening in the art pipeline, and don't be afraid to suggest your own fixes. Be clear about how much the change will impact the art team (or just yourself, if that's all you can speak for). Be very specific. Figure out how many extra minutes/hours/days you will have to add to your process. Ask if there is any way to automate the process so it won't impact individual effort.

Changes to Requirements Late in the Process

What it looks like: Art requirements get discussed and agreed upon up front, so everyone can create art that works for the final product. The art department gets started building art assets according to the plan. They bank quite a few and are right on target for completion. Everything seems to be going fine.

Then the rug gets pulled out from under everyone. The tech department insists that the requirements have to be changed. And they're

usually not requiring minor adjustments. The scale is entirely off, or the resolution has to be increased (or decreased), or the perspective is entirely changed. For instance, half way through production, the tech department drops the bomb that it turns out all the 3D assets have to have 25% fewer polygons.

This will require someone (or more than one someone) to go back to all that art already "completed" and make substantial changes—or throw out all that work entirely and start over. This is a major setback, and many times the programmers say something unhelpful like, "It's just a little change." Or maybe, "It's an easy fix."

What to do about it: First, assume good faith. The programmers may have found a big problem, and this is the solution they think will be best. They're not intentionally trying to make your life miserable. So begin by making absolutely certain you understand the new requirements. Sometimes the programmers will use art terms in unusual ways, and after a long talk, you will find out that they don't really intend the change to be as major as it first sounds. While you're having these conversations, avoid being confrontational. Assure the programmers that you want to help them solve this problem, but you need more information.

You may need to go as far as creating a piece of art under the new guidelines and making sure it works the way they intend. Don't think of this as wasted time or a wasted asset. This is part of the communication and problem-solving effort. It can help you find out (for instance) if they are talking about the texture resolution when they're saying "assets should be smaller."

• • • • • • • • • • • • • • • • • •
Lunch Topic

Ask programmers about what is most annoying, or aggravating about their jobs. Be there to listen to them while they vent, and pay attention to see if there is something you might be able to change about your own pipeline that could help.
• • • • • • • • • • • • • • • • • • • •

Once you have confirmation that they really intend the change to be as major as it first sounds, the next thing to do is to talk to them in their own language—with numbers. This will require some effort to do the translation, but it's essential for any kind of meaningful problem-solving to happen.

To translate this into numbers, first make an estimate of how long it will take for one artist (someone who works

at an average pace, not your fastest artist) to make the required changes to one art asset. This will be a painful process and it will feel vague. Some assets may take 10 minutes while others take 2 hours—or 2 days. Find a comfortable, realistic, average estimate and then multiply it by how many pieces of art are already "finished" according to the old requirements. Find out how many people-hours it will likely take for your art team to implement the changes. Don't exaggerate. It won't help. You may need to show them your math for them to grasp the size of the problem. If there are any places you skipped doing the actual math, the programmers will be able to discount your final numbers. Use the piece of art you made earlier that met the new requirements as your baseline example.

After you have translated the problem into terms, the programmers will understand and schedule a meeting with the head of the tech department and whoever else is in charge of the overall schedule (a producer, director, studio head, etc.). In that meeting, recap the required changes as you understand them. Make sure everyone is on the same page about what is happening. Then show your numbers and explain that because of this change your art department will require 6 more months to get the art to completion (or however long it is ... 2 weeks, 5 days, on projects with short timelines, even a few hours required extension can be a really big deal).

There are a couple of different ways this meeting can turn out. Either the change in requirements will stand or the tech department will be told they can't make this change because of how it will impact the final schedule.

If you "win" and the tech department is told they can't make the change, first of all don't gloat. This may be harder than you think. It can be a great relief to find out that you finally got your point across and were understood. But remember that by "solving" the problem for the art department, you've just created a big problem for the tech department. Before this meeting ends, offer genuinely and sincerely to help solve this problem. The change to the art requirements was almost certainly made because there is an underlying, even bigger problem. The change to the art requirements was the solution that came up with by the tech team. If you take that solution away from them, they still have that bigger problem to contend

with. Maybe it's a frame rate issue or an overall file size requirement. There are some hard limits the tech department can't negotiate with (for instance, if the distributor will reject any installer over this size limit). Programmers often can't think about other possible solutions until the one they came up with originally is proven impossible. Now that they have seen this solution won't work, they may be open and happy to have an artist brainstorm new solutions that work better for everybody.

If you "lose" in this meeting and the person in charge of the schedule puts their foot down and says this is the way it has to be, your next goal out of this meeting is to get more resources. If it's an extension on the art schedule, that's a win. If it's a promise to hire contractors or new permanent members of the art team, that's a win too. Just make sure you get some kind of change on the schedule since this has such a big impact on your team.

Changing Art without Talking about it Ahead of Time

What it looks like: Development on the product has been in full swing for quite a while. All the individual pieces have been getting attention from the most suitable specialist—art assets are being created by artists, while programmers hammer away at code. Just about the point where everything is being integrated for the first time, right when there are glimpses of the final product showing through the construction chaos, that's when this problem strikes. The programmers proudly show off the latest build—and the art is all wrong. Somehow, it's gone from perfect to perfectly dreadful. Something is wrong with the visuals, and it happened somewhere after it left the hands of the artists.

What to do about it: First, find out what happened. Don't make any assumptions about who did it or why. The first order of business is to understand what's affecting the way the art looks in the product.

This may be harder than you think. Keep in mind that everybody outside the art department doesn't look at the world the same way. They may honestly be unable to tell a difference between the art you submitted and the way it looks after it's been integrated into the

product. That doesn't mean the difference isn't real or important. Everyone has varying degrees of sensitivity to visual information, and some end users will look at the product (if it doesn't change) and feel like something is just "off." Even if they can't put their finger on what it is.

But you may begin with an uphill battle because the tech department may think there's no appreciable difference in the visuals. They honestly may not be able to see it. So your job is to examine the process. Just start asking questions. If you get any resistance, try to point out how the art is different from what you expected. Once you point it out, they may be able to see it. Especially if you place the in-product art next to an example that came off the art department desks.

If the tech folks can see the difference, they may have an idea of what is causing the problem. If they're still stumped, or just can't see what you're talking about, dig into the mystery yourself. Find out everything that touches the art or overlays it. Think about aspect ratios, pixel size (and shape), post-processing effects, and skew. Ask a programmer to walk you through the process of marrying the art to the tech. Did something get turned on inadvertently?

It's also possible the tech department knows exactly what is wrong with the art. It's possible they have done something intentionally to affect the way the graphics display in the product. In this situation, the most important thing is to try not to take it personally. Keep in mind everything written in the last two paragraphs about how the tech department doesn't look at the world the same way as an artist. What they have done to the art has little to do with the art itself, and everything to do with the problem of making their code work with your art. Sometimes a compromise has to be found, and that means both sides have to give a little. Ideally, this kind of thing is discussed before changes are made to the art by nonartists. But in reality, tech departments often think they are being more efficient by making a decision and moving on, rather than talking about it at great length. Efficiency is often the yardstick they measure by.

When you find the problem, whatever its source, communicate with the tech department about it. Show them what you've discovered, and why you think the original art is better. One of the three things will most likely happen next.

1. The tech department will consider it a bug and the bug-fixing process will get started. This is the ideal outcome from the artist's perspective, but it is also less common than the other options. So if you get this result, consider it a real win.

2. The tech department will consider it not a bug. They may even consider it essential to the function of the end product. This usually means something was unclear (or unknown) when specifications were communicated to artists at the beginning of the project. From the programmer's perspective, the art is the thing that is made incorrectly in this scenario. Even if the art follows the guidelines that were agreed upon in the beginning, the tech department will consider this an art problem if it interferes with the way their tech is intended to work.

   At this point, the best thing to do is to avoid pointing fingers or laying blame. It just doesn't really matter why or how this happened. What matters is what is going to happen next. So try to focus your energy on the here and now. Much of the advice in the previous section (Changes to Requirements Late in the Process) applies now. The short version is as follows:

   Make a piece of art that works with the tech using the new requirements. Cut down on the polygons, add more shadows, change the aspect ratio, whatever it takes. Make sure this sample looks correct in the functioning product, then determine if the art department has time to make these changes to every piece of art already created.

3. Regardless of whether or not the tech department considers it a bug, they may be unwilling (or unable) to fix it. They will think it's not important enough to spend any more time on. In this case, you have to decide if you can come around to their way of thinking. The best way forward is to start asking unbiased observers for their opinions about the art. Try to find people who are in the target demographic for the end product. Ask them if they see a difference in the art, and if they do, ask open-ended questions like, "So you can see the difference ... what do you think about it?" This will help to convince you or the tech department.

Pushing Solutions Off to Artists That Could Be Done in Tech (Animation, Color Changes)

What it looks like: The technology components on these projects are increasingly sophisticated. Whether it's a videogame engine or a website content management system, the tech has the ability to manipulate every element that goes into it—from changing all lowercase letters to all uppercase to effecting the antialiasing or putting in post-processing effects. The tech can change the art in good ways and bad. Nobody knows this more than the artists. Colors can be shifted, lines expanded, assets can be duplicated, and animations can be tweened.

So it can be extremely frustrating when the tech department dumps that kind of work back on the artists. It's tedious and reproducible. The perfect kind of job for a computer. Asking artists to do this kind of grunt work breeds a special kind of resentment. It feels like the programmers simply don't want to do the work, so they are foisting it off on artists they don't respect.

What to do about it: First, take a deep breath. The programmers are probably not intending to make any kind of comment about how much they respect artists. They just don't think that way. So don't ascribe malice. They're just being programmers.

What that means is that they probably have pretty solid reasons—though not always good reasons—for shifting the work away from their program and back into the hands of a human. Maybe the reason is that they don't like the quality of work the machine can do. Sometimes art really does need the touch of a human in order to look "right." They may have simply skipped communicating clearly—or showing you—how bad the art looked when the machine did its thing.

Case Study
Anonymous

Apple's graphics processing is bizarre and fascist. It requires ridiculous effort from artists. I've heard teams stumble over that before they figured out the res demands of the os and why their game was flat out breaking because a texture wasn't a power of 2.

I have the fortune of being most amused by my cofounder's reactions to what artists have to do without tools. "What are you doing?" "I'm just exporting all these sprites–" "you're WHAT?" "No it's fine it's only 62 steps–" "GOD. HERE. <makes tool>"

It's also possible the programming could do a fine job, but they don't have time to make it work. Every department has to make hard decisions about who works on what and how they can finish under time/quality/resource pressure. Maybe the one guy who knows how to make the tech play nice with the art is also the one guy who can make the menus work perfectly—but only if he focuses all available time on that task. Although programs can often do these tedious tasks, a programmer has to take time to make it work correctly. Some programmers can do that faster than others.

So when you can talk about the problem calmly and clearly, find out what was driving the decision to use manpower instead of tech. If you ask these kinds of questions when you're upset, it will likely come across as accusatory, which will put the tech department into defensive mode. You likely won't get a straight answer when they are feeling defensive, just excuses and attempts to shut down the conversation entirely. Nobody responds effectively when they feel like they are being attacked. So stay calm. Find out the thought process behind the decision to have artists do this particular work. It may help to get a project manager or producer involved to help sort out whose time is least available.

The answer may not go your way, but at least you'll know why a human needs to be spending their time doing a program's work.

Vague Change Requests (More Wow)

What it looks like: They say the art isn't right, but they can't say what's wrong with it. Vague or unhelpful words like "punchy" or "crunchy" or "upbeat" (all real words I've seen as suggestions to artist) are the substance of the feedback. Programmers are really hampered when it comes to talking about art. They simply don't have the vocabulary to express what they are thinking. So it often comes out in clumsy ways like, "It just needs more wow."

What to do about it: Build a shared visual language. Bring in reference images demonstrating changes that could be made to your art. Either make those images yourself or go the faster route and find images on the web to talk about. If the images you choose still don't seem right to the person giving the vague feedback, encourage them to find reference art online. When you find an image representing

what it is they are trying to explain, talk specifically about which parts of it they like. Your eye may catch on something entirely different than theirs does. So be sure you understand what part of their chosen image is the part they connect with. Try to build their visual vocabulary—but if that doesn't work, at least you'll have some idea of what they mean by "outrageous" when they use it in the future to request changes.

Arbitrarily Choosing Tech That Puts a High Burden on Art

What it looks like: Some decisions made by the tech department have ramifications on artists that are far broader and deeper than the programmers can imagine. For instance, deciding to use a complicated, unnatural perspective, or choosing to animate a horse instead of a car. Many times they characterize these changes as "minimal" or "easy" even though they have no real understanding of the impact on the effort involved for artists.

What to do about it: Educate them. Use numbers. Explaining how many hours will be involved in making one versus the other will help, but if there is a significant difference in the number of art assets total, that will be even more convincing for them.

Programmers may seem unsympathetic if you just say the decision makes things harder for you. Programmers tend to gravitate toward challenges and like to rebel against taking "the easy way." So they don't necessarily see something that is "hard" as being undesirable. That's not what you're trying to say, but it is what they are likely to hear if you try to describe it in those terms.

Most programmers strongly dislike tasks that are "time-consuming" or "simple/brainless but time-consuming." If that applies, try describing your problem in that way, and you'll likely get a little more sympathy.

Silence

What it looks like: The art department shows their work to the tech department and gets no substantive feedback. It could be a curt "looks fine" or no response at all. This can be irritating, considering

how much effort went into creating the art, but it can also be dangerous for the project, since it can result in change requests too late in the process, or development of assets in completely wrong formats.

What to do about it: Push to see the art incorporated into the tech. Many times the lack of feedback from tech departments really means they haven't tried using the art assets, and so don't feel like they have any feedback to give since it hasn't been married to their efforts yet. They don't usually have the ability to imagine the art in context. Without seeing the art inside the program, they often don't have a frame of reference to evaluate it. So encourage them to incorporate it into the product as soon as possible. It's likely when they take this step, they will have plenty of feedback, so be ready to listen.

Lunch Topic

Bring a variety of pictures with you to lunch and ask everyone—programmers and artists alike—to describe the images. Get people talking about any emotions the images evoke, but also start introducing concepts like contrast, hue, and light. Point out similarities and differences in the way words can be used to describe very different images.

Working on Unimportant Tasks Instead of Key Issues

What it looks like: You can't make progress until tech figures out some key specifications and/or methods, but that task never makes it to the top of the priority list. The programmers are constantly working on other tasks, potentially making progress on their own endeavors, but hampering yours.

What to do about it: Remind the tech lead that the artists are stuck and can do nothing more productive than play wastebasket basketball. Explain why the artists are waiting for this piece of the tech, and ask if there is anything the art department can do to speed up the process—researching specifications on similar products or creating sample art in a range of specifications so they can try different pieces to fit into the puzzle.

Many times the task is being delayed because they get laser focused on their own goals and forget that their efforts could be hampering other departments.

Occasionally, the delay is necessary because the part that will let the artists move forward literally cannot be built without the other pieces in place. If that's the response from the tech department, you'll have to trust them—even if it seems unlikely in your experience. The fact is that you have the tech department, and if they say they can't do the job any other way, they really can't. If you remind them that the artists are having fun and goofing off while they're slaving away, they may be motivated to think of another approach that could get the artists working sooner, but it will usually be taken more kindly if you offer to try to help with the task instead of flaunting the fact that you're waiting for them.

Promising Tools that Never Materialize

What it looks like: Programmers often have big ideas about programs they can write to simplify or speed up common tasks. Sometimes these ideas will get codified into specific plans to make tools to help artists. Many times they are very helpful tools. Unfortunately, they often remain vaporware—much talked of, but never delivered.

What to do about it: Don't count on it. Never build your pipeline around a tool that doesn't exist. If the tool is completed before the rest of the project is, then you can incorporate it into your process. However, no matter how enthusiastic the programmers are about making this tool, prepare for life without it.

For one thing, tools break. So even if the tool gets delivered, it may go down on the same day the creator is out sick. Artists need to know how to make progress on the end product without any specialty, homegrown tools. It's a risky thing to have in the pipeline.

Many times they're valuable tools that save hours of artist effort, and losing them for even a few days can be a big setback, but knowing the process to keep going without them will make sure the art department isn't entirely shut down by something they're not responsible for.

Keep in mind that programmers like side projects just as much as artists, but it's often hard to justify working on code that won't end up inside the final product. There always seem to be higher priorities focused on the end product—the thing people are paying for. Tools can speed up the process, but they are often seen as "nice to have"

rather than "must have." It can often help move production of the tool along if you can quantify exactly what they will do. Once again reduce the process into numbers—hours worked, time spent waiting, or numbers of assets touched unnecessarily. Project managers can see the trade-offs more clearly when they can compare two like things—number of hours artists spend on this process versus number of hours a programmer would spend to cut that first number in half.

Silos, Hoarding Information, and Internal Competition

What it looks like: Programmers getting very upset when someone in the art department touches programming in any way—building a time-saving tool, adding a post-processing effect, particle effect, etc. Even if everyone agrees the end product is great, the tech department may get very angry about artists stepping on "their turf" and refuse to allow the art-created "tech" into the final product. They actively harm the project as they defend their territory from the encroachment of people on their own team.

What to do about it: Involve the tech department as soon as possible. Don't surprise them with how great the tool works, instead talk to them about what you would like to try before trying it. If there is internal competition in the organization, it will raise its ugly head here, and with the help of leads and project managers, you can combat it in the early stages before it harms the project.

Some of the best ways to break down silos is to break down the physical barriers that are emblematic of the workflow silos. If you have any control over seating arrangements, consider integrating artists and programmers together into the same workspace. Alternate seating, or otherwise ensure artists are sitting right next to programmers on a daily basis, not just in an artist-only pod. Allow feature teams

Case Study
Anonymous

I once made an access database to coordinate art production with writing. It worked really well, and I did it so the data could be exported into the full game engine.

When the tech director saw it, he went ballistic. Apparently he thought I was making the tech department look bad.

with representatives from multiple departments to sit together. If you don't have control of seating arrangements directly, try making the suggestion to those who do.

Alternatively, when you're working on something coming close to tech's "turf," take a laptop over near their workspace while you work on that feature. Being physically close to them, asking their opinion, may help them see you as a member of the team, and not an enemy at the gates.

Finally, don't fall into this trap yourself. Artistically inclined programmers may create effects, animations, and other assets that fall into artistic territory. Bite back your instinct to take offense. Remember that you're all on the same team, working together to make the best end product you can all make. It may seem like commentary or criticism about how you're doing your job, but most of the time, those programmers are only trying to help and not trying to show you up at all.

3 The Way We Think

The Programmer's Mind

The mind of a programmer is never quiet, but usually it's an organized kind of activity. Things in their head are fairly linear and have a structured format. It may feel a little jumbled to them, but compared to an artist's mind, it's very orderly.

One of the things programmers and artists have in common is that they like to do a lot of conceptual work. Before a project starts to take shape in code, they organize and think it all through. They may skip over some parts that need to be fiddled with, but they usually have an overall schematic in mind when they sit down to start writing code.

This is similar to the way artists brainstorm and maybe even sketch different versions of an image before they begin to create it. There are several ways to approach every coding problem, but programmers like to have a complete vision of how they will build their code before they ever begin. This is a very creative part of their job, and they dislike having that creativity overlooked or underappreciated. Writing code is not easy. It requires ingenuity and thoughtfulness in its creation. The end point may seem like a simple feature, but the route to get there can be quite challenging and unique to the individual programmer, just like brushstrokes and individual style for an artist.

These similarities can be one way artists and programmers connect. Recognizing the creativity of their jobs—rather than treating them like a machine where ideas go in and working programs come out—can be a foundation of commonality and respect between the two disciplines.

● ● ● ● ● ● ● ● ● ● ● ● ● ● ● ● ● ●
Lunch Topic

Ask programmers if they think of their job as creative work. Find out how much they do conceptually before they start typing. Ask them if they can see a program in their head before they write it. Look for similarities in the way you work, for instance, conceptualizing an image before sitting down to draw.
● ● ● ● ● ● ● ● ● ● ● ● ● ● ● ● ● ●

While programmers think about programs in ways that are familiar to artists, the biggest difference is in the tools they use to get the concepts out of their minds and into the real world. While artists struggle with imprecise tools that don't always do what the artist wants, programmers work with a toolset that is very black and white. Either a program runs and does what they want it to or it doesn't. The personal style and expression is all hidden in the code behind the program. Different programmers may take different routes to the same end point, but that end point either does what the program needs to do or it doesn't.

While artists are sometimes frustrated with their tools doing things they hadn't quite intended, programmers are faced with tools that always do exactly what they're told, nothing more and nothing less. This means they can bring what's in their mind out into the world with a higher degree of fidelity ... but it also means that if something goes wrong, it goes very, very wrong and it's often difficult to find the problem.

A programmer doesn't have to deal with their creation taking on a life of its own and going a different direction than anticipated. Rather, they have tools that are so black and white that they either work as intended or not at all. A little eraser around the edges won't bring it back into focus. If the program doesn't run, that means somehow, somewhere the programmer made a mistake. And yet, it's not that something sloshed a little in application. The program only does what the programmer told it to do. So even if they have it figured out conceptually, it can take a while to make sure the code says what the programmer intends it to say.

Case Study
Mike Sellers, Creative Director

In one of our project courses here at IU we had a young programmer who was rated poorly on his peer reviews by the others on his team, while he had given himself high ratings. We discussed it (privately) and walked him through the others' views. The fortunate result was that by the end of the semester his peer review scores were much better, and he's been on a couple of teams with some of the same people since.

He said at the time that this was the first project where he'd had to work closely with nonprogrammers, and now he really understood that they simply think *differently* than he does, and that those differences are necessary for making a good game. My response was that if he could learn that at age 20 rather than 30 or 40, he was going to do all right.

And then, when it does function, it usually has to work together with portions of the larger program that other people wrote in different ways, and this can sometimes lead to unexpected interactions. While artists know that mixing yellow and blue will result in green, a coder doesn't know for sure what will happen when his code mixes with someone else's on the team.

So while coding is an act of creation as much as a piece of art is, the uncertainty in the process is in a different place than it is for artists. Art develops gradually, starting out in a rough stage and coming along until it meets the needs of the project—and hopefully the original concept the artist started from. A program starts out feeling complete and perfect to its creator, then they face a lot of outright rejection as they try to find the things they mistyped that are keeping it from running, or the ways someone else's code works with it differently than they expected. Rather than getting gradually more and more satisfied with their work, they often start out confident in their product and then gradually get less and less positive feedback, less and less evidence their idea was a good one.

Because of this, many programmers develop a tough skin and an attitude of absolute certainty that can come across as overbearing, undeserved ego. But usually it's the only way they can make it through the final stages of the coding process as they have to have

faith in their own work even when an entire team of bug testers are telling them it's all wrong. If they lose that confidence in their ability to code, programmers wouldn't be able to push through the negativity at the end of the process to the point where it does what they knew it could do all along.

④ Providing Feedback

How to Give Feedback to Programmers

Programmers think in very concrete ways. Many times, something that looks like it's broken to you will actually be functioning as intended by the programmer. They are usually ready to admit and accept that something is broken. They will be eager to get in and fix any bugs. (If they have time at that point. Schedules can be tight, but programmers are usually very conscientious about providing bug-free code.)

It can be more difficult to convey to programmers that something they made technically bug free is still "not working" for the overall project. If they respond to feedback by saying that this feature is "functioning as intended" that means they think the problem is with the specifications for what they were asked to build (or with frequently changing specifications), rather than the problem being with the actual thing they built. This may feel like pointless blameshifting, but for programmers it's personal. They spend just as much time trying to read other people's minds as artists do, but instead of vague artistic descriptions like "happy and fun," they will get incomplete specification lists and vague design documents.

Also, they won't always be able to see the difference between art provided and art displayed in the software. They haven't been trained

to see all the individual elements that go into making a piece of art look the way it looks. So, if the shadows are showing up 20% lighter than they should, they may not even see that there are shadows, let alone that they are different from the art provided.

- Use verbs. Talk in terms of actions and behavior of the software.

- Explain step by step what you were expecting to happen, as you show them what actually happens. Methodically walk through the steps of using the software to show the difference between what was expected versus what is happening.

- Choose specific elements of the art you can point to as showing up differently in the software.

- Ask questions about why something is showing up different from how you expected, not in an accusatory way, but to demonstrate that you are interested in helping to solve this problem, if only you knew how.

- Find examples of software that behaves in the way you expected. Show them in the context of explaining your expectations, not in showing them up as unable to solve a problem other people have solved.

- Make sure you're both on the same page about how the software is supposed to perform.

- Use numbers, if you can, to quantify differences between expectations and reality. Sometimes it's as easy as pointing out that there are supposed to be three lines showing, and instead there are two. More often, it's a question of polycount, frame rate, or antialiasing.

5 Taking Feedback

How to Listen to Feedback from Programmers

Sometimes it's hard to take feedback from programmers. Programmer art is notoriously … basic. They generate a few different colors of squares and call it good. However, when the art department burns the midnight oil for 3 weeks, the response seems to go one of the two ways—indifferent shrugging of the shoulders, or nitpicky criticism.

It's hard to hear negative feedback from people who can't draw a straight line. It's very easy to respond with something snarky like, "Oh yeah? If it's so bad, why don't you come over here and fix it?"

This probably won't foster a positive working relationship, however. The key is to listen to their feedback not as you would take it from another artist—rather, think of these comments as coming from the end users, the people who will ultimately be interacting intimately with your artwork.

Case Study
Anonymous

Programmers got into a heated debate with the artist doing the box art for the game; the artist wanted screen and asset captures at 300 DPI. Programmers asked what resolution. Artist said, uh, 300 DPI. The disconnect lasted over a surprisingly high number of exchanges.

Programmers can't see the world the way artists can, but neither can most of your users. The people using the software every day may not be able to tell the difference between cyan and puce either. These aren't expert opinions you're hearing when you talk to programmers about your art, but they are usually honest, unvarnished reactions you may hear from your audience.

Ask questions: Even if their feedback seems pretty clear on the face of it, ask clarifying questions to make sure you're both on the same page. One person's "gritty" is another person's "grungy."

Take notes: This will make the programmers feel like you are really hearing what they have to say, even if you don't end up doing what they suggest. If you write down their feedback it will feel to them like you gave their opinion a fair chance.

Take some time: Don't rush back to your desk to implement all the changes you talk about instantly. Let it sink in for a while. Talk it over with other artists. Go back to the programmers and ask clarifying questions later if you realize something was vague or could be interpreted two ways. This is another reason to take notes. It gives you a great reference for dealing with the feedback after the initial sting has worn off.

Listen for the message: Programmers often don't have very strong social skills. Many times they don't think carefully about how they will word feedback. Their first thought is what comes out of their mouths. Sometimes this makes it a little difficult to hear what they're really trying to say. Abrupt, harsh criticism hurts. The pain of it can cloud out the underlying point the programmer was trying to make. So, do what you can to look past the general delivery and tone. Programmers mean well, they just don't have a lot of interest in verbal delicacies.

Assume good faith: Everyone is on the same team, and everyone wants to make the best product possible. No matter what the tech department says, they don't really want to destroy the art department. They want beautiful art. They just have no idea how to get there. (If they did, they would be the art department.) This doesn't mean their opinions are invalid. In fact, they care much more deeply about the end product than impartial observers. So, no matter what it sounds

like on the surface, they do want the art to be the best it can be. To hear what they are really intending to get across, you need to start with the assumption that they mean well. Even if the words they're using don't make it seem that way. Their focus is on the product, not on the feelings of their teammates.

Ask them to show you what they mean: Many programmers won't have the vocabulary needed to express what it is they're trying to get across. Not all of them will think of using a visual example to help communicate what they mean, so ask them if they can show you an example or two from other work you've done or from other products. Sometimes when they're complaining about the shadows, they really mean that the light is too bright or too direct. (Or not direct enough.) They often don't know what it is that seems off. They just know something isn't sitting right. Pictures can keep you from spending a lot of time on the wrong thing.

Don't do all the talking: It's tempting to defend yourself when negative feedback comes in. This usually backfires if it happens in feedback sessions with technical people. Even if it's a very rational explanation of the limitations of the system, the technical person will often tune out and wonder why you asked for their opinion if you were just going to ignore it. You may get plenty of feedback that doesn't apply because you're working toward a goal set by someone higher up or because you're working under constraints of accessibility (colorblindness) or competition (we can't use our competitor's color scheme). Don't volunteer the explanation for why things look the way they look. If the programmer asks why, go ahead and explain, but remember you are here to listen, not to lecture.

Be kind: Sometimes the reason for the art not meeting expectations is a technical one. For instance, the programmers have limited the color pallet, or fixed the aspect ratio. This can be uncomfortable, and it would be easy to point fingers right back at the tech department when this happens. However, it would be more productive to listen carefully to the feedback—then agree with them. Speak in terms of wish lists and added features. For instance: "You're right. That would be great. If we had another sixteen colors to work with we could have a more gradual gradient. But we'll see if there's anything we can do to smooth it out with the constraints we have." Sometimes a

comment like this will open the eyes of the tech department to just how much they have constrained the art department. If they don't change the constraints, they will at least be more sympathetic to your problems. (Because they are likely working under similarly uncomfortable constraints themselves.)

Say thank you: Feedback can be hard to hear. It often feels like a long list of inadequacies and personal attacks. Regardless of how it's delivered, say thank you—sincerely—to the person who provides the feedback. You want to hear about problems before the product is released to the public. You want to know how you can improve your collaboration and your craft. You want friends and colleagues to push you to be better. So even if it feels painful and awkward at the time, be sure to thank the person who took the time to help you understand how the art looks to fresh eyes.

Although feedback from programmers can be hard to interpret, sometimes it's even worse to have silence as the only response to your hard work. Some programmers feel like they are so unqualified to critique the art, they simply never speak up. If your programming department is giving you the cold shoulder (and you'd like that to change) here are a few techniques you can try:

Show and tell: On a regular basis, invite the programmers into the art department for a "show and tell." Make it a quick, fun presentation of the artwork you're most proud of for that week (or month, or day). After the presentation, encourage discussion. Seed a few people in the audience who are comfortable giving feedback, and ask them to get the conversation started. A simple, "That's what we did this week. What do you guys think? Are we mostly on track? Anything looking like we've gone too far with something?" Have someone ready to take notes and follow up if more detail is needed from someone who is a little shy about commenting in a group setting like this. Even if there's little to no discussion, a presentation like this can set the groundwork for hallway conversations or the ideas listed below.

One-on-one sessions: Schedule short meetings (15 minutes or less) with the tech leads and ask them pointed questions about their opinion of the art. Provide a quick presentation if a larger one hasn't already been given. Then genuinely listen to their feedback and ask questions. Keep the sessions short. Programmers often feel like they

are wasting their time if they aren't actively writing code. These sessions are critical for art departments sometimes, but the tech department often doesn't see how or why they matter. Don't worry about trying to explain it to them (unless they're interested) just focus on keeping the meetings short. Especially don't go overtime by explaining away or making excuses for any critique they do give you. They will often feel like that means you don't really want to hear their opinion.

Bring in bagels, or go out for pizza: Bring in a box of bagels or donuts for the tech department specifically, then hang out near it. When people walk up to get a pastry, make small talk about the art. You may be surprised at how freely programmers talk when they've been encouraged with a little food.

 Giving It Back

Communication Is a Constant Looping Cycle

Now that you have feedback from the more technically inclined section of the team, what do you do with it? It's awfully tempting to ignore it completely or follow it slavishly. Frankly, either way is the easy way out and probably won't help.

Consider the two options. If you're going to ignore the feedback, why go to the effort of asking for it in the first place? Even if it doesn't seem helpful, useful, or remotely pertinent, it is an additional information. It's more than you had before. No matter what it is, you can find a way to make good use of it.

On the other hand, following the feedback down to the letter will paradoxically often lead to disappointment from the very people who provided that feedback. They're counting on you to inject your skills and talent into the fix. If they could make the changes themselves, they would have.

Many times the people who are providing feedback can see problems or concerns—but they don't know how to fix them. Even if they say they do. The fact is that they are providing feedback on a unique piece of work created by an individual who is not them. This work has hidden elements and motivations they have no idea about. The changes they are proposing or problems they are highlighting are

Case Study
Mike Sellers, Creative Director

The art lead and the tech lead were having all kinds of difficulties. It turned out the root of it all was Git. The programmers loved it, the artists loathed (and feared) it. The programmers had also unilaterally instituted a file naming scheme that worked for them in Git, but which the artists found incomprehensible, and so they ignored it. The overall result was that a lot of art was in a parallel ad hoc version control "system" (sorta), and was named along an evolving scheme the artists came up with that worked for them, but which had also changed over time. It was a long difficult road to get everyone on the same page, including getting the programmers to understand that no, they didn't get to unilaterally decide such things, and the artists to understand that yes, they really did need to have versions of their art organized and available to others. Eventually, we got it all worked out.

unique to how they are seeing the creation. This is inherently not the way the creator sees them.

But this doesn't mean you can wave them away with a "you just don't understand me." You can do that on personal projects where the end goal is self-expression alone. But in a group effort with an intended audience in mind, feedback about places where the message is muddy or confusing is invaluable. Art communicates, and it does so no matter what technology it's paired with. If that art isn't communicating the right message, or as effectively as it could be, changes need to be made so that it can speak clearly.

Accepting this reality is the first step to take after hearing feedback from the tech team. They see with such different eyes—eyes that most of the audience will also be seeing the art through—that their responses and explanations about what the art is doing can be lifesaving for the art. Much better to hear now, during development, that something has gone awry than after launch when the audience comes back with "I don't get it."

The second thing to do after accepting that the feedback is useful, valid—and yet, not an iron mandate—is to try to articulate back to the person who gave the feedback what it is you heard them say. Make it a conversation. This is about making the product better, not about anybody's ego.

So, make sure that you repeat back to the person giving the feedback what it is you heard them say. Dig down underneath the surface of their words and ask if you heard the heart of it correctly. The miscommunication inherent in speaking different languages using the same words can mean that you heard one thing and they meant something entirely different.

Sometimes this conversation has to happen with pictures included. So, if the feedback is that the art is "too dark" try making a change—reducing shadow effects, increasing contrast, removing some gritty textures—pick one, apply it, and take the results back to the person giving the feedback. Tell them that you understand the previous version was "too dark" and ask if this new version has addressed the problem.

Don't spend too much time on this initial effort. It's entirely possible that you will adjust the contrast and they will respond by saying that the look on the character's face is "still too brooding." What you want to know is if you have correctly interpreted the feedback. This only requires changing one asset (or one small set of assets in some cases). It's a huge waste of time and effort if you make the changes to everything and then find out you misunderstood the original problem. So start small.

When showing your trial effort to the person who gave the original feedback, try to express to them what you heard them say—without using their own words. So, if the feedback was, "it's too dark" you might say something like: "What I got from our feedback session was that the art was too muddy. It didn't have enough contrast. So I made some changes. What do you think?" You may find out that what they meant by "dark" was something more like "dystopian or gritty" and it had nothing to do with the contrast.

Try not to be accusatory or defensive. Stay professional and matter-of-fact. Here are some phrases to try:

- What I got from the feedback session was ....

- I heard that there was a problem with ....

- When I took a long look at the feedback, I saw ....

- In the feedback session, I heard ....

A good rule of thumb is to try to avoid using the word "you" because this isn't about the other person at all, really. This is about the effect their words had and the images their words conjured up. Focus on saying "I heard" or "I saw" or "I learned." That way you're not accidentally sounding petty or accusing, as you can if you say, "You told me this ...." or "You said I should make this change."

Feedback should be a constant, looping cycle with the product moving in a spiral upward, constantly improving as the give-and-take of the feedback loop makes it better and better.

7 Professional Courtesy

How to Treat Each Other Professionally/Well

Art never feels like a team effort. It's personal. It's intense. It takes individual courage. But on projects that require a whole group of people, you're not in this alone. In all the good and bad ways, you've got a cadre of people there to make comments, throw wrenches in the works, and work beside you to the bitter end.

It can help if you think of it as a party—either of the adventuring type or the cocktail type. You don't get to invite just the people you want to be there, but you need everyone to act in a fairly civilized manner if you're going to get out the other side with the equipment intact.

Don't forget that they're counting on you, just as much as you're counting on them. You're all in this together. With that in mind, here is a list of things you can do to build confidence with people on the team who are not speaking your language. These are little habits you may not see as important, but they can help smooth the way immensely when working with people who are different from you.

Be reliable: This applies to both punctuality and output. Being on time for things is often not at the top of the priority list for creative people. Being ready feels more important than being on time. However, for most people who are not us, being on time is essential.

They see it as a matter of respect. Many people would rather have you there on time and unprepared, than late and well-prepared. It's just a quirk of how their brains work, and instead of fighting against it, trying to make them see sense, this is usually one of those battles it's not worth fighting. Being on time—to meetings, with deadlines, in every way—is a small price to pay for peace and respect from your teammates.

Just as important is to be consistent with the quality of your work. Even on elements or assets that are not as fun or interesting to work on—put in the same quality of work you do on the rockstar elements. This doesn't mean gold plating the berries on the bushes. Everything needs to be the level of quality it needs to be, and if you can show that you understand where that level is—and can deliver on it consistently—your team will trust you. That is priceless.

Communicate clearly about problems: The only way to manage "Be Reliable" is to also "Be Transparent." Realistically speaking, deadlines slip and traffic backs up, and now and then you'll be running late. Make every effort to build in a margin of error, a cushion for these times when things don't go your way. But also start communicating more about how things are going, both positive and negative.

If you realize you're going to be late to a meeting—send a text. If you're going to have to bring a sketch instead of a finished piece, let everyone know that ahead of time. It will probably feel like you are "oversharing" but you probably aren't. Just make sure you're not phrasing the communication in terms of an excuse or complaint. It's just a status update.

When working in teams like this it's important to provide a sense of how the project is moving along, even if it's not a piece that directly impacts our section of it. When a person or department goes dark, the rest of the team is left to fear the worst—that no work is getting done at all. So frequent status updates, both good and bad, can be your best friend on a team. It shows you're being proactive, and can cut off at the pass any suggestion from other departments that

• • • • • • • • • • • • • • • • • • • •
Lunch Topic

Ask programmers if there are parts of their jobs that are boring and repetitive. Ask them how they handle those tasks, and share strategies for staying focused for the un-fun parts of your jobs.
• • • • • • • • • • • • • • • • • • • •

a meeting must be called (taking you away from your work) so that they can find out what the current state of the project is.

It is possible to become a pest with these updates, so do ask for feedback from the people you're sending them to. Make sure you're updating them the way they want to be updated.

Ask questions: Be interested in the overall product. Even though your own piece of the effort may seem to be the icing on the top, and your teammates may minimize what you do as "easy," showing interest in what your teammates are doing is just polite, for one thing. For another, it can help you do your job better if you have a deeper sense of how the rest of the team is doing and what they're working on.

Ask questions about how things work. Show interest in the pipelines and processes. Make sure you understand the final goals. Even understanding the monetization methods can help you make the right pieces of art draw the right amount of attention.

Don't interrupt other people when they're in the zone, but show interest in their part of the project. When you send out status updates, ask pleasantly how things are going for your coworkers. And if they respond, show interest in what they have to say. You're all in this together, and if you ask the right questions you can also head off a lot of problems before they get too big to manage.

Remember it's not personal: Programmers tend to be blunt and somewhat lacking in social graces. Sometimes their feedback may sound like a personal attack. They may word things such that it sounds like they don't like you as a person, rather than having a concern about assets fitting together.

No matter what they say, your job is to keep it professional. Try to let the personal comments roll off your back. Focus on the project and how your material fits in. They may be trying to articulate a very valid concern, but doing it in a clumsy way. Try to listen past the attack and hear the heart of the issue.

Give your best effort—if you're not happy, it shows in your work: One of the unique things about working as an artist is you can't plow through your day being miserable and still be productive. You may create a lot of art when you're buckled down and unhappy, but you'll likely have to do it over again. Your attitude shows in your work.

When the artists aren't happy, the art may be technically appropriate, but artistically disappointing.

So, if there are things about your job that get under your skin—addressing those issues can solve art problems. Don't phone it in. People will notice.

 Danger Signs

Warning Flags That Communication Is Breaking Down

O ne of the most challenging parts of a communication problem is identifying when misunderstanding has started, but not blown up into an obvious crisis. The very nature of miscommunication is a circumstance where each party believes they are understanding and communicating clearly, when in fact something important has been misconstrued or misstated.

As long as everyone believes they are communicating well, the problem goes undiagnosed until it reaches a crisis. On team projects this is usually the point where the end product begins to take shape in some tangible form. When words have been translated into actions, misunderstandings have moved from internal misinterpretation to external, visible examples.

If you can catch the communication problems before too much work has been done, more time and effort can be spent working in the right direction, and less time fixing and reworking.

So, how do you know there has been a communication breakdown? Often you'll have a nagging suspicion or gut feeling, but tech-minded people have their own unique symptoms. Any of the following attitudes could signal an underlying problem.

Many assurances that everything is fine ... but no evident progress: If progress reports are all words and no demos—that's a sign that there may be a problem. For instance, if the art department has been churning out assets which the tech department says are "fine," but you're not seeing those assets show up in the product yet—that can signal a big problem.

Of course, it can sometimes take a little time to get past placeholder assets to using the real thing. Don't be too quick to worry here. A few days to a week is a normal delay between turning in final assets and seeing them incorporated into tech. Any longer than that, however, can indicate there is a big problem brewing.

The source of this is usually overconfidence. Someone somewhere is so confident about the art guidelines provided upfront, that they haven't bothered testing it yet, because of course theoretically it will work perfectly, slotting right in where it's supposed to go. But reality and theory are sometimes miles apart. Things change from the initial design concept. People interpret guidelines and specifications differently. They have to be tested to see how things work together—the sooner the better.

So, start asking to see finalized art assets incorporated in the working version of the product. It may help to phrase it as wanting to make sure you followed the specifications correctly. Insist that seeing it in a working version of the product will make a big difference. It will.

Many times the tech department won't even notice if something is being stretched or skewed. They won't realize the color is being pushed too far into the blue side. They just don't have the artistic eye. If they did, they wouldn't need artists. So, make sure you can see your work incorporated into theirs, and raise questions if things don't look the way you expect them to.

And if you're not seeing finished art showing up inside the working version of the product, start fixing the communication channels immediately.

Case Study

Anonymous

In a big, AAA game, we were well into production and the artists were creating character models and animations, but the AI programmers were taking forever to determine what actions would be possible for the characters. We couldn't work on animations beyond the basic walk, run, jump for way too long.

The programmers did not believe that they didn't have the entire product schedule to figure out the AI actions that were going to be in the game. The designers had given them a prioritized list, but the programmers refused to commit to how many they would be able to support. We had to go back and redesign levels to take away actions that we thought the NPCs were going to eventually be able to do.

In addition, the programmers refused to give the artists a ball-park figure for the polygon budget. They were locked in analysis paralysis and wouldn't even give a floor. It was frustrating as hell.

Repeating the same suggestions or feedback over and over: Another sign that something might be wrong with your coworkers over in the tech department is when they start to sound like a broken record. They may come over to the art department and say exactly the same words, or redeliver exactly the same memo they gave you earlier. When they are repeating themselves, it's a sign that something has gone awry.

Tech-minded people often have a very limited vocabulary when it comes to aesthetics. When they start repeating themselves, it probably means they are trying to say something different from what you think they are saying. The same way Americans sometimes try to communicate in other countries just by speaking English louder. They are feeling like their message is not getting across, so they're trying again … just not in a very helpful way.

The first step to combating this problem is to say back to them in your own words what it is you are hearing them say. Ask them if you're understanding them right, but try not to use the same words they have been repeating—those words likely don't mean what they think they mean. Ultimately, the fastest way to move communication along if it's stuck in a rut is to show them some art and ask if that art fits the specifications.

Translate the words into actions, something tangible, as soon as possible, and get immediate feedback about it. If they're repeating themselves, you're missing something.

Repeating the same policy reminders over and over: This warning sign is similar to the previous one about feedback, but instead of focusing on something about the art assets, the repetition is all about processes and policies. Maybe it's file naming conventions or approval checklists. Whatever it is, the tech department just keeps talking about it, over and over.

This probably means they think something important isn't happening the way they need it to happen. There may be something you're inadvertently skipping, or have numbers switched around or something. They may be the ones who have forgotten to write down a step or a number or explain something fully.

The important thing to remember is that when the tech department starts repeating themselves, it means there is something being misunderstood—either by them or by you. So if something is getting repeated, make sure you walk through the process or procedure with them standing there looking over your shoulder to check and make sure you are doing what they think you are doing.

Constantly changing requirements and specifications: Just as irritating as the broken record can be when the goalposts keep moving. There will always be some adjustments that have to be made as the plan starts to become a reality, but if there is just one adjustment after another, with a new set of specifications every 10 days or so, something has broken in the communication lines. One or two adjustments to specifications are inevitable, but if they keep changing it's entirely possible the communication of those specifications is as much of a problem as the specifications themselves.

Anytime art specifications are discussed, always provide sample art that meets those specifications so that they can be tested.

Not talking to anyone about anything: It's easy to think that "no news is good news," and to a certain extent that can be true. Everyone needs to stop talking at some point and get working. So, sometimes radio silence can be a great sign. However, if the tech department

isn't talking to anybody about anything, that's a sign that they've run into a roadblock and they're stuck.

There may be something the art department can do to help. It's possible the original specifications for art assets are causing part of the problem. If you can get a tech person to talk through the issue, there may be some change the artists can make to alleviate the roadblock.

However, it's just as possible the problem has nothing to do with art. The tech department may appreciate a sympathetic ear. It can still be very helpful to talk through a problem, so don't think of it as a waste of time. If you open up the communication lines during this slowdown, they will be more likely to talk through problems art can help with later on.

If any—or several—of these are happening right now, it's important to try to repair the broken communication lines. Chapter 9 focuses on how to do that, but it may also be useful to look at previous chapters to get a better understanding of where the problem started. Technically minded people view the world from a different vantage point. Something on your side may have inadvertently triggered an avalanche, or the tech department may be struggling to communicate with you in your language. Recognizing there is a problem is the first step.

 # Mending Fences

How to Talk about Fixing a Broken Communication Line

When communication breaks down, someone has to make the first move to fix it. Giving the cold shoulder may make you feel better temporarily, but it won't solve problems or make life any easier at work. Eventually, someone has to be the grown up and it might as well be you.

Have a Meeting

Get a meeting on the schedule to talk about communication. Be clear that's the purpose of the meeting, and keep control of the agenda so it doesn't get pulled off topic. Try to invite those in leadership and project management roles. If for some reason that's not going to work—scheduling nightmares, for instance—have the meeting with anybody who will show up. The communication has to start somewhere. Nobody can do better at communication all on their own. There has to be someone to communicate with.

When writing the agenda, make sure it's clear that you intend to make changes yourself. Be careful about providing an outline that only suggests changes in other departments. Acknowledge that it's a two-way street and that you would like to know what you can do to improve.

Keep in mind that you genuinely want to know if there is something you or other artists are doing to shut down communication. Finding this out would actually be a huge benefit. It would mean that the problem is within your power to fix. You won't have to be persuading, encouraging, and hoping that other departments will make changes in the way they communicate. If you find out that the problem is on your end, you can make the changes yourself.

Share the agenda with everyone invited to attend. This way they can come prepared to talk about the right subjects. They can also decide if someone should be added—or subtracted—from the invite list to make it a more productive meeting.

Many times, these meetings don't need to be a company-wide affair. It's often best to start with those in leadership positions so that people can have more frank and open discussions.

Provide Lists of Bullet Points

Once the meeting starts, provide bullet points for each agenda item. Agenda items that are too vague can lead to communication wandering in circles instead of moving toward productive conclusions.

For instance, "Art/Tech miscommunication" does describe the problem, but it doesn't help define it. It doesn't give anyone an entry point to grapple with the problem. So bullet points like this could get things started in a more productive way:

Agenda

Art/Tech miscommunication

- Examples of miscommunication

- Consequences of miscommunication

- Causes of miscommunication

  - Listening?

  - Clear messages?

Solution brainstorm

- What can art do to improve?

- What can tech do to improve?

Be prepared to let the other side vent a little. Let them suggest solutions. Don't try to dictate what they will do in the future. Ask nicely and be prepared for pushback.

Be specific: Programmers think in very concrete terms. Words like "always" and "never" are taken literally, not just as a sign of how frustrated you are. They will often get sidetracked thinking about exceptions to the rule, instead of the problem you're trying to tackle.

Bring concrete examples with you. Don't be afraid to name names if it helps, but at the same time, remind everyone that these are specific examples of larger problems. Be clear that you're not blaming the participants, rather that you'd like to use these examples to help diagnose the larger problem. More than one example, involving different people, can help others spot trends. So try to talk about multiple, specific instances where the communication problems were most apparent. This isn't about throwing anybody under the bus. It's about taking a vague complaint about coworkers and looking at it as indicative of attitudes, processes, or applications of policies.

Try this: Take responsibility. If there are things you or your team have done—good reason or no—that contributed to the problem, fess up to it and say you're sorry. It can even help to give a blanket apology for your part in the communication problem, even if you haven't figured out what your part is yet. Simply acknowledging that you're not perfect can help other people in the meeting feel like it will be safe for them to admit fault as well. And even if it doesn't go that far, you taking responsibility for your part can at least open a door for your colleagues to talk about ways you can improve your communication skills.

Avoid this: Don't place blame. Even if the problem is almost entirely one-sided, or lies squarely on the shoulders of one person, it won't be helpful to make that person feel ashamed or guilty. Those feelings will more likely lead to resistance and defensiveness, rather than

true change. So avoid placing blame. Instead, acknowledge there is a problem, but focus on how information could be communicated differently.

If someone never reads emails, ask if a text would be better. Maybe having it printed on a piece of paper and left on their chair? A personal conversation and action items written down by pen? The point of this meeting is not to drag anybody over the coals. The point is to find new ways of communicating.

Try this: Recurring meetings. Get regular feedback sessions onto the calendar, but make them friendly, fun events. Talking more frequently can nip problems in the bud and make course corrections gradually instead of in landslides. If the tech department is hesitant about coming, find out what you can do to make the meeting more useful or enjoyable. Would it help to make popcorn or bring donuts? It's a small price to pay.

Avoid this: Meetings where nothing happens. Start meetings by showing the impact their previous comments made. Show how you are using the feedback. If they feel like the meetings are unimportant or skippable, they will be skipped.

Try this: Written surveys. Sometimes programmers will freeze up if asked a broad question like, "What do you think of my art?" They don't have the vocabulary to describe what they're thinking. Consider giving them that vocabulary in survey form. It may feel silly at first, and don't shy away from making the event feel light-hearted. Programmers sometimes worry that they'll say something wrong. Multiple choice questions, entered privately on their own survey form, can feel like a lot less pressure to them.

Treat it like a game, though, and not like a high-school quiz. Make it clear that there is no "right" answer. You genuinely want to know their opinion.

Avoid this: Putting them on the spot. Programmers often need a little time to figure out how to talk about art. It grows on them over time. Don't keep your art secret until the moment you ambush them

• • • • • • • • • • • • • • • • • •
Lunch Topic
Ask programmers about how they get feedback or critiques of their work. What kind of feedback do they think is helpful? What is not helpful?
• • • • • • • • • • • • • • • • • •

looking for an immediate response. Put your art up on the walls of the hall they walk down. Hold "show-and-tell" sessions where they are invited to look at what art was done this week, but hold the feedback for later.

Try this: Figure out very specific questions you want answers to. "Does this art asset fit the overall product vision?" That's a question everyone is qualified to answer. "Is this art at least as good as our competitors?" Sure, that's subjective, but it will provide ample discussion points. It will also provide a framework for feedback, rather than throwing the door open for unhelpful or vague responses.

Avoid this: Don't expect programmers to behave like art critics or even art students. They've never been in an art critique session. If there are customs you like to employ when talking about art, make sure you explain those customs to your coworkers.

Try this: Suggest small changes. Every little bit helps. So if you can just get programmers to stop saying, "This art sucks," and start saying, "I don't think this fits our vision," count that as a win. Go for small, incremental steps toward a larger goal of better communication. Focus on steps made and not on how far you still have to go.

Avoid this: Don't demand overnight miracles. People are the way they are. They don't change easily. Keep this in mind, and celebrate small victories. If people promise to do things differently and then don't, remind them gently about their promises, and thank them for whatever changes they did manage to make. It can be a long process as everyone finds new ways to work with each other. Be patient with them.

10 Eating Crow

How to Apologize and Make Friends if Something Goes Wrong

Nobody's perfect. Mistakes happen. Communicating is hard. It's really more unusual when things go right with no hiccups, than when there are bumps and wrong turns. Creating anything as a group effort is very difficult.

So if communication has broken down, or a crisis has arisen because of a misunderstanding, the best thing to do is work together to fix it. Accept things didn't go perfectly and make two plans—one plan for fixing the current situation and one plan to avoid getting off track in a similar way in the future.

When you're ready, sit down with everyone affected by the problem and start with an apology. Yep, a good old-fashioned apology, for the part you played in the situation. You can do it. It won't kill you, and it will smooth things over with your colleagues. Starting out this way will get them thinking about ways they could have done things differently as well. It will help. Nothing else will work as well.

Before you head in to make an apology, take a few minutes to focus on unrelated things you do well. It's easier to apologize if you remind yourself that the area you messed up in is not the only thing that defines you.

Don't skimp on your apology. Make it real and sincere. A real apology has all these parts, usually in something close to this order:

- Say you really are sorry. Use the words. The important point to get across is that you regret what happened.

- Show you understand what happened from their perspective, but be careful not to make it sound like the problem was all in their heads.

- Make it clear that you made a mistake. Take responsibility for the action that caused problems.

- Outline a realistic plan for moving forward. Include ways you will avoid the miscommunication that started it all.

- Promise to do your part to make this plan a reality.

Don't dwell on the negative. Once the apology is made, move on. Programmers, just like other human beings, appreciate hearing a sincere apology, but they appreciate even more seeing real changes. So don't keep referencing the mistake, just get busy doing the things you promised to make things better.

Programmers usually appreciate ongoing changes in behavior rather than grand, but temporary gestures.

# Programmer Dictionary

Disambiguating Words Tech-Minded People Use

This dictionary won't help you decipher every word programmers ever say to each other. That jargon takes years of practice and training to understand, and they almost never expect people outside their departments to pick up on all of it. They are usually quite willing to explain any programmer lingo they use with each other.

The real miscommunications happen with words nobody thinks about as jargon. These common English words seem like they should have pretty much the same meaning to everybody. But they really, really don't. These small misunderstandings can snowball into a lot of confusion.

This dictionary focuses on the implicit meanings programmers are usually intending to convey when they use these common words. Many of the meanings are different from what artists expect, but it's not that either side is wrong about how they use these words. They often just don't realize they are using them in a jargony kind of way. So this is where you can go to check the meanings of these innocuous-looking troublemaker words. They don't intend to do harm.

3D—adjective or noun

What programmers may say: *"Can't we make this more 3D?"*

What programmers usually mean: This is one area where some programmers are inadvertently less technical than artists. There are programmers who specialize in graphics programming and know a lot about 3D rendering. However, this is a very specialized field. Many programmers often talk about 3D when they want something to have more perceived perspective or depth.

What programmers don't necessarily mean: This should be modeled and rigged in 3D software.

Bright—adjective

What programmers may say: *"I need to make that brighter."*

What programmers usually mean: Programmers may not be trained to see the difference between brightness, contrast, saturation, etc. When they say "brighter," they might mean more light, warmer colors, more contrast, and less muddy. They understand it at the level of lights turning on after dark, but they often don't understand the subtle effects light (simulated or real) can have on color or texture. If a programmer asks about the brightness of something, be sure to ask more clarifying questions.

What programmers usually don't mean: They often don't know how much lighting can affect art. They will often focus on making things visible, rather than thinking through how the lighting will change the mood. It's just not something they think about.

Color Wheel—noun

What programmers may say: *"Why do you keep bringing up the color wheel?"*

What programmers usually mean: They usually think of the color wheel in the "color picker" tool palette. Programmers usually think of it in terms of choosing individual colors or adjusting shades, not as an organizational methodology for choosing color schemes and understanding relationships between opposing colors.

What programmers don't mean: *"Stop talking about making things look good."*

Contrast—noun

What programmers may say: *"I need to add more contrast here."*

What programmers usually mean: The difference between two things needs to be highlighted or exaggerated. This could mean adding a black line between them or making one brighter or larger. They are thinking about emphasizing the differences between things when they talk about contrast.

What programmers usually don't mean: The tech person's definition of contrast is usually quite broad. They sometimes react to the artist's definition as being too constrained and technical to the point of jargon. Neither side is necessarily wrong on this.

Cool—adjective

What programmers may say: *"This fire is very cool."*

What programmers usually mean: This looks good. It's very trendy.

What programmers usually don't mean: *"This color leans toward the blue side of the color wheel, and that's a bad thing."*

Depth—noun

What programmers may say: *"These stairs need more depth."*

What programmers usually mean: They need to fundamentally change the shape of this object. If the programmer has graphics training, they may think of "bit depth" as it relates to digital images—how much information can be used to display the image. However, they generally use the phrase "bit depth" instead of just "depth."

What programmers usually don't mean: Doesn't refer to "deep colors" like dark brown or black. Doesn't refer to texture or richness. Refers only to physical depth of an object, either modeled or implied through perspective.

Easy—adjective

What programmers may say: *"That will be easy."*

What programmers usually mean: They understand how to achieve the thing being asked of them. It seems straightforward, considering what they know about the problem and the context at this time. This doesn't usually mean it's trivial or simple or quick, just that it's understood. There is also a high likelihood that a programmer who identifies something as easy will also get that thing done, whether it's a high-priority item or not, but they may put it off until the last minute as they prefer to work on problems they think they understand less. See "Trivial."

What programmers usually don't mean: *"That won't take much time."*

Feature—noun

What programmers may say: *"I need a list of features."*

What programmers usually mean: Programmers think of features as all behaviors, not as a list of adjectives and adverbs describing the software. "Easy to use" and "intuitive" are not features of a program in a programmer's world. They are marketing copy. Programmers look at a list of features as a to-do list of items they have to build. So a feature might be "player character can jump" or "user can change the volume with a slider." They consider all the functionality to be features.

What programmers usually don't mean: Anything important or highlighted.

Finished—verb or adverb

What programmers may say: *"I'm finished with that project."*

What programmers usually mean: Although this can vary from studio to studio, often when a programmer uses the word "finished," they mean the conceptual phase of the project is finished. They may not have written any actual code yet. To outsiders, this may look like the project hasn't even begun yet, but remember that the tools they

use to get the conceptual work out of their head and into a functional piece of programming are very black and white. Things either work as intended or they don't. If they don't, there are established problem-solving processes to bring it into line. In many ways, the writing of code is the very last stage of the programming effort, not the first. Arriving at a common definition of "finished" can be a very useful exercise for teams trying to work together.

What programmers usually don't mean: The task is completed, tested, and ready to ship.

Functioning as intended—adjective

What programmers may say: *"That isn't a bug. It's functioning as intended."*

What programmers usually mean: The behavior, which has been identified as a mistake or a bug, is actually working the way the programmer intended it to work. So it's not really a mistake on the programming side. If there is a problem, it's with the original design of the feature or with some other interlocking piece. It's kind of like saying that this piece of art may not be to your individual taste, but it is what the specifications called for. As an artist, you may agree it's not entirely to your taste either, but regardless, that's what you were asked to produce, so you did. That's what "functioning as intended" means to a programmer, and it can be a frustrating situation for everybody. Just like with art, this can happen when the specifications are unclear or if a larger communication problem is muddying the waters. So when this comes up, making sure everyone has the same vision for the product can be an important next step.

What programmers usually don't mean: *"Not my problem."*

Hot—adjective

What programmers may say: *"This corner is hot."*

What programmers usually mean: Programmers almost always use the word "hot" in the casual slang sense of trendy or awesome. They will tend to think of it in terms of actual temperature, and not as a technical term for intensity or color.

What programmers usually don't mean: *"This corner is too bright or intense, or red."*

Midnight—noun

What programmers may say: *"We'll move everything over at midnight Thursday."*

What programmers usually mean: Computers think in terms of numbers and aren't very good with nuance. People who work with them get very good at thinking in specific terms. This shows up starkly in conversations relating to time. For computers, and programmers, midnight is the first minute of a day, not the last. So midnight Thursday is right after 11:59 p.m. on Wednesday. Programmers also frequently use a 24-hour clock or "military time," so if they are talking about something happening in the afternoon, it will be 14:30 for instance (2:30 p.m.). For them, this removes ambiguity without requiring more characters.

What programmers usually don't mean: They don't mean to be stubborn about this. It's just what they're used to.

Model—verb

What programmers may say: *"We could model that."*

What programmers usually mean: Create a simulation or calculate what will happen.

What programmers usually don't mean: Sculpt this in 3D software.

Modular—adverb

What programmers may say: *"I thought this was supposed to be modular."*

What programmers usually mean: Modules in a program are sections that can be moved around independently, changed or recoded internally, taken out and used in other programs, and only the inputs and outputs have to stay the same. They are very flexible. Programmers will often think of art the same way if it is described as modular. They will often think the pieces are totally malleable

and assume they can change aspect ratios, dimensions, and colors without having a negative impact on the overall look.

What programmers usually don't mean: People who are not artists don't usually assume that digital modular pieces shouldn't be changed (stretched, shrunk, etc.) to fit whatever circumstances arise.

Network—noun

What programmers may say: *"You want to network this?"*

What programmers usually mean: Programmers normally think of the network and networking in the technological sense of two or more computers communicating with each other.

What programmers usually don't mean: Human interaction or cooperation.

Numbers—noun

What programmers may say: *"Your numbered list makes no sense."*

What programmers usually mean: Programmers start counting with 0 because computers do, too. That's how computers work. They aren't joking when they start a numbered list with zero, and they don't intend for you to skip any step listed as zero. Many times, they remember this is a quirk of talking to computers so much, but now and then, they slip up and begin with zero on humans.

What programmers usually don't mean: *"I'm being intentionally obtuse."*

Paint—verb

What programmers may say: *"Can't you just paint this red?"*

What programmers usually mean: Many programmers use the word "paint" to mean changing colors over broad areas—like painting with a room in a house with a roller or using the "paint bucket" tooltip in simplified image software.

What programmers usually don't mean: *"Make this look like it has brush strokes."*

Perspective—noun

What programmers may say: *"We might need to change the perspective."*

What programmers usually mean: Often programmers use the word perspective to mean "viewing angle." So changing the perspective would mean moving the camera from over the shoulder to overhead.

What programmers usually don't mean: When programmers use this word, they are usually not talking about the many ways of showing perspective well-trained artists are familiar with.

Repurpose—verb

What programmers may say: *"I just repurposed your art over here."*

What programmers usually mean: They reused art assets, possibly by changing their size, aspect ratio, or orientation. Programmers often don't have the visual training to notice something looking incorrect when it is squeezed or stretched.

What programmers don't (necessarily) mean: "I duplicated art assets but didn't modify them."

Resize—verb

What programmers may say: *"I'll just resize that piece."*

What programmers usually mean: They will enlarge or reduce the asset until it fits the space required, but won't make adjustments to the resolution. They may also change the aspect ratio without realizing it. Tech people won't necessarily notice (or care about) any stretching, blurring, or muddying as a result.

What programmers usually don't mean: They don't usually think of the effort that goes into making a polished asset in several different size versions. They often won't notice problems of scale on trim, wood grain, etc. It's not intentional, they just don't notice, and when it's pointed out to them, they often argue that since they didn't notice it, the products' end users won't notice either. This is probably true to

a certain extent. Players who are like them won't notice. Players who are like you will notice. So don't let the programmers convince you it's not important. If it changes the way something looks, it's worth fixing.

Resolution—noun

What programmers may say: *"What do you mean the resolution is wrong? It's the same everywhere."*

What programmers usually mean: Programmers tend to think of resolution as applying to monitors and windows as a whole. They often don't think about how it applies to individual assets, created independently, then integrated into the whole.

What programmers usually don't mean: They're not playing dumb or trying to be difficult, they just don't think about how artists work.

Stretch—verb

What programmers may say: *"Yeah, I stretched that a little to fit. What's the big deal?"*

What programmers usually mean: People without a great deal of intimate experience with digital art assets are often not aware that changing aspect ratios will have a significant impact on how the asset looks. They will often increase one dimension without increasing the other dimension, and not notice that is appreciably different. Or they will increase both dimensions, but by different amounts. They often think getting close enough is fine and aren't trained to realize maintaining exact aspect ratios is important.

What programmers usually don't mean: They often won't think about taking the asset back to an artist to rework the asset to the new size.

Shrink—verb

What programmers may say: *"Yeah, I shrunk that a little. I still think it looks fine."*

What programmers usually mean: Similar to the problem of stretching, shrinking doesn't always mean someone has changed

the aspect ratio. Sometimes, they just change the size of the asset in relation to other assets (especially if they have gotten in trouble for stretching things previously). However, they don't change the resolution or textures to fit other assets.

What programmers usually don't mean: They don't mean to do it on purpose, and often can't see the difference. They may think it looks a little different, but don't think it's a big deal. They're not trying to make you crazy.

Tile—noun

What programmers may say: *"Is that going to be tile?"*

What programmers usually mean: They may think first of tile as the building material, as square pieces with lines of mortar between them.

What programmers usually don't mean: They often don't think about the complexity involved in creating a seamless, repeating pattern.

Trivial—adjective

What programmers may say: *"Oh sure, that's trivial."*

What programmers usually mean: They often say something is trivial if they think of it as both easy to implement, and won't take much time to complete.

What programmers usually don't mean: This is unimportant.

Value—noun

What programmers may say: *"What's the value there?"*

What programmers usually mean: When programmers use the word "value" they are usually expecting the answer to come in the form of a number. When used in relation to color, they expect the RGB hex values. They aren't usually trained in color theory. For programmers, they more commonly refer to variables having values. Mathematics uses the word value as well.

What programmers usually don't mean: Value as it relates to color theory.

Zero—cardinal number

What programmers may say: *"We're going to start at zero."*

What programmers usually mean: Computers start counting at zero, so programmers tend to do the same. It's such an essential part of how computers work, it becomes a habit to start everything with zero, even though they also agree that it means "nothing."

What programmers usually don't mean: They don't usually mean to be difficult or snide when they start numbered lists with zero.

Programmers Index